KU-513-292

VEGAN
LIFE

Cruelty-free Food, Fashion, Beauty and Home

JO PETERS

summersdale

VEGAN LIFE

Copyright © Summersdale Publishers Ltd, 2019

All rights reserved.

No part of this book may be reproduced by any means, nor transmitted, nor translated into a machine language, without the written permission of the publishers.

Vicki Vrint has asserted her moral right to be identified as the author of this work in accordance with sections 77 and 78 of the Copyright, Designs and Patents Act 1988.

Condition of Sale
This book is sold subject to the condition that it shall not, by way of trade or otherwise, be lent, resold, hired out or otherwise circulated in any form of binding or cover other than that in which it is published and without a similar condition including this condition being imposed on the subsequent purchaser.

An Hachette UK Company
www.hachette.co.uk

Summersdale Publishers Ltd
Part of Octopus Publishing Group Limited
Carmelite House
50 Victoria Embankment
LONDON
EC4Y 0DZ
UK

www.summersdale.com

Printed and bound in the Czech Republic

ISBN: 978-1-78783-016-5

Substantial discounts on bulk quantities of Summersdale books are available to corporations, professional associations and other organisations. For details contact general enquiries: telephone: +44 (0) 1243 771107 or email: enquiries@summersdale.com.

Neither the author nor the publisher can be held responsible for any loss or claim arising out of the use, or misuse, of the suggestions made herein. Consult your doctor before undertaking any new forms of exercise or making any significant changes to your diet.

CONTENTS

INTRODUCTION

Vegan Living

There's never been a more exciting time to explore a vegan lifestyle, and it's easier to follow one now than ever before. Vegans choose to avoid any products that come from (or have been tested on) animals, which is why all vegans follow a plant-based diet. This has numerous health benefits – and is much less harmful to the environment – but for most people, choosing to avoid animal-based products is an ethical decision: the peace of mind that comes from living a compassionate life is the greatest benefit of all.

But avoiding animal-derived food and drink is just the beginning. Sadly, animal products may be used in the production of everything, from toiletries to furniture, but with a little thought it's possible to make careful, cruelty-free choices when shopping for all sorts of items and clothing, too.

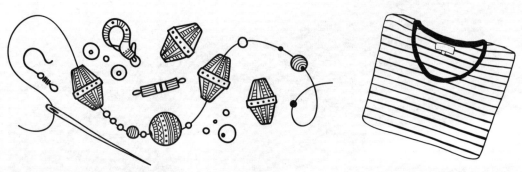

This book shows you how easy it is to enjoy the benefits of a vegan way of living. Veganism is not about restricting yourself to eating a few bland salads or whittling your wardrobe down to a pair of canvas shoes. It's about trying out wonderful new ingredients and flavours, feeling energised and healthier than ever, meeting like-minded souls and lessening your footprint on the Earth. With tips on the best ways to transition to a vegan lifestyle, easy on-the-go recipes and practical ideas for making your own vegan products, *Vegan Life* includes everything you need to know to make your choices as cruelty-free as possible.

Whether you're exploring veganism for the first time or looking for some extra tips, you will find all the information and inspiration you need to embrace and enjoy your vegan life.

Note: Oven temperatures given for the recipes throughout the book are for fan ovens.

CHAPTER ONE

WHY VEGAN?

Veganism is...

Veganism is not about self-denial – it's about making positive choices, and opening yourself up to a host of new tastes and experiences. When you choose a vegan lifestyle, you are choosing:

- ✦ To ensure that no animals are exploited to provide you with food

- ✦ To eat a diet packed with flavour and vitamins

- ✦ To discover new and exciting cruelty-free foods

- ✦ To feel – and look – healthier

- ✦ To have more energy

- ✦ To join a community of compassionate, caring individuals

- ✦ To select products that have been created in an ethical way

- ✦ To leave a lighter footprint on the Earth

- ✦ To respect all living things

- ✦ To experience peace of mind by living in the best way you can

- ✦ To discover new places to eat

- ✦ To live in harmony with the world around you

What's not to love?!

 # THE HEART OF THE MATTER

For the majority of vegans, the choice to avoid animal products is an ethical one. Veganism is about extending our natural compassion for living things to those animals that are used in the production of foods and other goods: creatures just as intelligent, loving and characterful as the companion animals that we nurture and build relationships with at home. The reality of how livestock are treated, transported and slaughtered is difficult to contemplate, but it is often what motivates a move to veganism. There are many good documentaries that cover this in more detail (see p.156).

Approximately 60 billion land animals and over a trillion sea creatures are killed for food production every year.

Everyone who chooses to eat a plant-based diet makes a difference. If you eat a vegan option three times a day, every day, then after a year you will have clocked up over 1,000 animal-free meals. And even if you decide to just eat vegan occasionally each week, your choice will lessen the demand for animal produce. Remember also that every time you pick a vegan option when you're out and about, you are influencing the people around you.

Depending on your current diet, you could save between 100 and 200 animals every year by going vegan.

What about Free-range and Organic Farming?

Unfortunately, no animal reared to be slaughtered has a good quality of life or is allowed to live as long as it could. In reality, organic and free-range farming do not live up to what we are often led to believe. For instance, free-range chicken and egg production results in many 'free-range' chicks never seeing the light of day or surviving past their first few days.

EATING GREEN

Choosing a vegan diet has far-reaching benefits for the environment and the whole planet, as animal agriculture uses so many more resources than the production of plant crops. The rearing of cattle and other livestock demands enormous quantities of food, water and energy, as well as using vast swathes of land.

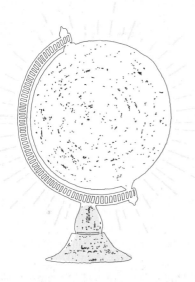

Land

Animal agriculture and growing plants for feed take up 33 per cent of the Earth's land mass, and an amount of land equivalent to around seven football fields is bulldozed every minute to make room for farm animals.

A typical omnivore's diet demands five times more land than a vegan's.

Water

It takes 300 gallons of water to produce food for a vegan for one day, but 4,000 gallons for a meat eater – that's the equivalent of 95 bathtubs full to the brim!

Greenhouse Gases

Livestock and their by-products account for 51 per cent of all worldwide greenhouse gas emissions, which is four times as much as transport emissions.

By giving up meat, you'll be doing more to reduce your carbon footprint than by giving up your car!

Wildlife and Ecosystems

Animal agriculture has a major impact on ecosystems and is a prime cause of species extinction. It also leads to deforestation and, as a result, flooding. (Removing trees reduces the amount of rainwater absorbed and intercepted, causing increased run-off and soil erosion.) Additionally, livestock grazing is the number-one cause of plant extinction.

Fish

Overfishing causes habitat destruction and decimates fish populations. Many sea creatures – including whales, dolphins, sharks and turtles – are killed as by-catch, having been trapped in fishing nets and discarded. Around a quarter of all fish caught (and farmed) are used to feed livestock, rather than humans.

It's easy to see why many scientists believe that eating a vegan diet is the single most effective way of reducing our environmental impact on the Earth.

A Healthier Way to Be

A well-balanced, plant-based diet has many health advantages over one that relies heavily on meat and dairy products. It cuts out the high cholesterol and other nasties that are part and parcel of the typical omnivorous diet. Also, when we base our meals around a variety of fruits, vegetables, nuts, grains and pulses, we are naturally getting the wide range of vitamins and minerals that we need to keep ourselves in tip-top condition. Our body works better when we eat in this way because we're fuelling it with more accessible nutrients, including all the fibre that we need.

Animal-based Diet	Plant-based Diet
Contains cholesterol	There's no cholesterol in plants
High in saturated fats	Low in saturated fats
Low in fibre	High in fibre
Products contain animal growth hormones (which may cause cancer) and antibiotics	Contains no hormones or antibiotics, most plant-based foods are highly nutritious instead!
Linked to high blood pressure, heart disease, cancer, diabetes and Alzheimer's disease	Linked to lower blood pressure, and far fewer incidences of these diseases
Products contain bacteria, which can cause E Coli, Salmonella, etc.	Not present in the majority of plant-based foods
Tend to be higher in calories; can lead to weight gain	Lower in calories; can help you to achieve a healthy weight
Poor source of vitamins and minerals	High in essential vitamins and minerals (if you eat a good variety of foods)

If you're eating a balanced vegan diet, you'll soon notice that your body is functioning – and looking – better than before. Without animal products taking a toll on your system, and *with* a wide variety of accessible nutrients on hand, you'll be amazed at how much healthier you feel. Here are some of the benefits you might experience:

- Better concentration
- Peace of mind
- Shinier hair
- Fewer headaches
- Improved eyesight
- Fresher breath
- Enhanced sense of taste
- Reduced body odour
- Reduced irritability
- Improved immune system

- More energy
- Clearer skin
- Stronger nails
- Fewer food cravings
- Fewer PMS symptoms
- Less bloating
- Regular pooping
- More stamina
- Healthier weight

Super Side-effects

A vegan diet can improve or even clear up long-term medical symptoms, but food is often surprisingly left out of the equation when you consult a medical professional. The situation is changing, though, and you can find doctors who are well-versed in plant-based nutrition (see p.155). There's a lot of research focusing on the link between nutrition and disease, and the evidence points to the fact that a plant-based regime can help to prevent illnesses such as cancer, heart disease and Alzheimer's disease. Even sufferers of conditions such as diabetes, high blood pressure, depression and MS have seen improvements in their situation when switching to a vegan diet.

According to a British Heart Foundation study published in 2018, a vegan diet can reduce premature mortality by 18–24 per cent.

Be Prepared for...

As with any diet alteration, you may experience some changes while
your body adjusts to your new eating regime. These will usually
stop once your digestive system has adapted to eating a higher-
fibre diet and you get your calorie intake right, but do check with
your doctor if any of these symptoms persist or are worrying you.

- ✦ Acne
- ✦ Wind
- ✦ More frequent trips to
  the bathroom than usual

- ✦ Headaches
- ✦ Hunger
- ✦ Fatigue

And remember: if you feel hungry, eat! Vegan foods tend to be lower
in calories, so you may need to eat more often and include some
extra snacks in your day, to make sure you have enough energy.

If you currently have a medical condition or illness, do check with
your doctor before making any lifestyle or dietary changes.

SUPERFOOD FIX

As a vegan, you'll be basing your meals around nature's finest nutrients. In fact, if you eat a balanced vegan diet, you'll be getting a fix of the superfoods that nutritionists have identified for their amazing properties, including:

Avocado

A vegan's best friend, these fruits are packed with beneficial nutrients, including folate (which protects us against digestive cancers) and a wide range of vitamins.

Berries

Antioxidant powerhouses that boost the immune system with vitamins and fibre, berries can also reduce levels of 'bad' cholesterol in the body.

Leafy Greens

Super-nutritious, they protect against chronic illnesses, packing in vitamins, minerals and antioxidants. In particular, they're a good source of calcium and iron.

Mushrooms

Nutrient-rich, anti-cancer foods that are produced in an eco-friendly way, too. They contain B vitamins and are a good source of antioxidants, including selenium.

Nuts and Seeds

Full of omega-3 fatty acids, which support good heart and brain health.

Pulses

A rich source of protein, fibre and vitamins, they reduce cholesterol.

Seaweed

A great source of vitamin K and iodine (especially beneficial to vegans).

Sweet Potatoes

Rich in many nutrients, and the carotenoids they contain are great antioxidants.

Turmeric, Ginger

... and other spices are anti-inflammatories that are effective in preventing illness.

Nobel Prize-winning biologist Elizabeth Blackburn studied the effects of a vegan diet and found that – in just three months – many genes causing disease were switched off, and those preventing disease were switched on.

🌱 AN EASY CHANGE

Changing to a plant-based diet is easier now than ever before. Thanks to the huge increase in **vegan products** out there, you can buy (or make) almost any dish that an omnivore would eat. You can find **vegan food on planes** and **trains**, and vegan options in **restaurants** and **coffee shops**. Thanks to improved **food labelling** – and useful apps – it's easy to check whether the items on the **supermarket shelves** are vegan friendly. When you factor in the support and knowledge of the **vegan community** (both online and in the real world), you can see how easy it is to make the change and open up to a world of **innovative ingredients**, **creative recipes** and **cruelty-free products**.

It Doesn't Cost the Earth

Thanks to the rise in specialist vegan products on the market, you'll find yourself spoilt for choice when shopping. But these options can be pricey, so remember that at heart a vegan diet is based around fruit, vegetables, nuts and grains. None of these things are expensive – unlike meat and cheese! – so don't feel that you need to shell out on specialist goods when you can easily prepare vegan food at home for a fraction of the cost.

MAKING THE MOVE

There is no single right way to transition to a vegan diet: some people like to make the change overnight, but for most a gradual approach works best. You could start by replacing your foods with vegan options when they run out: experiment with soya and nut milks or give meat replacements a try, for example. Another approach is to adapt one meal at a time across the week – breakfast is an easy place to start – or why not go vegan for one day out of seven? (Pick a day when you aren't under pressure and have time to prepare new dishes.)

If you're fired up and ready to go all-out vegan overnight, be sure to plan ahead. You could sign a pledge with one of the vegan societies online to get plenty of support and have access to web resources that will help you to stay motivated and on track (the Veganuary campaign is a good example).

The word 'vegan' was invented in 1944 by the founder of the Vegan Society, Donald Watson, who felt the need for a term to describe someone who used no animal products at all. He said that the word vegan – taken from the first three and the last two letters of 'vegetarian' – marked 'the beginning and the end of vegetarian'. (Other words considered were 'dairyban' and 'benevore'.)

 # TRANSITION TIPS

Learn All you Can

Check out your local vegan or health food stores and any vegan restaurants in the area for inspiration; buy magazines on the topic and join online forums to learn practical tips. Vegan festivals are a good place to pick up information, meet like-minded people and try different foods.

Plan Ahead

Check out the essential nutrients you'll need to include once you're eating a fully vegan diet (see pp.36–37) and get a few basics in your store cupboard. Read the ingredients lists on products you've already got at home and learn how to spot non-vegan ingredients (see pp.44–45). Plan ahead for any meals out that might be coming up in your transition period, too.

Add to your Diet First

Get used to eating more pulses and beans, nuts, seeds and tofu, so that you're familiar with how to prepare them, before you cut down on other foods. If you take it one step at a time, you won't feel too overwhelmed.

Find Some Favourites

Find some simple but tasty recipes that appeal to you and get used to these first. You could look up a vegan version of whatever your favourite meal is at the moment – there's one for every dish you can think of, so you won't be disappointed!

Take it Easy

Start by cutting out the things that you'll miss least first and when you get to the tougher options, remember that there's a vegan alternative for almost everything; it's just a case of finding what suits you best.

Think Positive

A positive attitude is the best thing you can take with you on your vegan journey. Focus on the fact that you're exploring new options and discovering a whole new healthy way of living – you're not going on a diet or restricting yourself to a few bland meals. And don't be too hard on yourself if you make a few mistakes at first. You're still a vegan, even if you slip up!

Breaking Down the Barriers

If there's a non-vegan food you think you'll find tricky to give up, leave it to the end of your transition. Then make a deal with yourself to cut it out for three weeks and see how you feel at the end of that period. If you still have cravings, try a vegan alternative first. If you do decide that you just can't manage the full transition, don't give up on your otherwise vegan ways! It's much more beneficial to be as vegan as you can – with the exception of the odd non-vegan food – than to go back to a fully carnivorous lifestyle.

FRIENDS AND FAMILY

Food is at the heart of most family get-togethers and it won't be long before you find yourself reassuring your nearest and dearest that a vegan diet will provide you with all the nutrients you need. You know your reasons for going vegan better than anyone, but remember that you don't need to get drawn into lengthy discussions about nutrition or animal welfare if you don't want to. You can simply reassure your loved ones that you've done plenty of research and know that a plant-based diet is the healthiest choice for you. The best way to get your family on side is to show them how veganism suits you. And it doesn't hurt to take a few tasty vegan offerings along to the next gathering, of course!

Mini-vegans

If you're raising mini-vegans, rest assured that it's absolutely possible to do so while providing them with a balanced diet. Do your homework and make sure that your little ones are getting the nutrients they need, including supplements. Also remember that growing kids need more calories – a vegan diet can be high in fibre and leave children feeling full before they've got all the energy they need – so offer them bananas, hummus and nut butters, as well as lower-fibre carbs such as white bread or rice. Talk to your GP or a paediatrician for advice before you take the plunge.

OK. But where will you get your calcium?

Calcium-fortified plant milk, spinach, kale, broccoli... in fact, lots of vegetables are great sources of calcium. Animal products only contain it because the animals have absorbed it from plants: by eating veggies, you're going straight to the source! And don't let anyone tell you that it's not possible to maintain healthy bones on a vegan diet... At least not without you mentioning the fact that some of our planet's largest land mammals do just that.

What about protein, though?

With beans and lentils, nuts, soya milk and tofu, it's easy to get your daily recommended allowance of protein. Moreover, plant proteins are much better for us than animal proteins, as plants are packed with nutrients but include none of the cholesterol.

Won't you miss out on iron?

Nope! Lentils, chickpeas, cashew nuts and seeds are all good sources of iron. You can impress your family by explaining that – as iron is absorbed more easily when eaten alongside vitamin C – you like to include a good source of that at the same time, by adding broccoli to your stir-fries or drinking orange juice alongside your muesli.

But won't you miss desserts?

Not at all – there are more vegan ice-creams, cheesecakes and decadent puddings out there than you can shake a spoon at. (You might like to take along a couple of options for your loved ones to try.)

LIVING WITH NON-VEGANS

Whether you're living with a non-vegan flatmate, partner, parents or siblings, sharing with someone who doesn't follow your lifestyle choice can seem like a bit of a challenge, but there are plenty of things you can do to make the transition easier for your household.

House Rules

It's best to have a chat and establish some house rules as soon as possible: have a think first about the areas where you might need to find a compromise. Here are some examples.

- Will you be happy to prepare meals that include animal products if you regularly cook for others?

- When storing food, would it be possible to have a separate area of the fridge – or even a mini-fridge – for non-vegan produce?

- Are you happy to share cutlery and crockery with your housemates?

- Can you agree on a totally vegan day at least once a week?

- Will you be able to encourage them to use vegan cleaning products?

Once you've given these areas some thought, have a chat and find the solution that suits your household best.

Lead by example, rather than trying to convert everyone under your roof to veganism through hard-line activism(!) – especially if it isn't something they've considered before. If you regularly eat together, take the opportunity to cook up some of your tasty meals: a hearty vegan chilli in the slow cooker for everyone to dip into at the end of a long day won't go amiss (see p.68). You could also surprise your housemates with a breakfast of vegan pancakes and maple syrup (see p.48) or some freshly baked vegan cookies (see p.65).

If you have a partner who isn't vegan, don't see this as an obstacle to your transition – plenty of households need to adjust to different dietary needs at mealtimes and it's

perfectly possible to accommodate both your diets. You might prefer to cook only vegan foods – big stir-fries or veggie dishes with mashed potato, for example – which your partner can eat as sides and supplement with separately cooked meat or fish options, if they wish. Eating out together at a restaurant that serves really tempting vegan fare is another great way to showcase how tasty a vegan diet can be.

Staying Motivated

Adapting to a vegan lifestyle can feel like a big step at first – particularly when you're still getting to grips with what you can and can't eat – but keep these tips in mind and you'll be ready for the doubts or dips that might crop up in the first few weeks.

✦ Remind yourself of why you're vegan: you could even write down a personal statement of what veganism means to you and carry it with you.

✦ Make a list of motivational clips/memes on your phone.

✦ Remind yourself of the health benefits by writing down the changes that you've already noticed.

✦ Read inspirational stories online from other vegans to help you stay positive.

✦ Remind yourself that veganism is not complicated. It's a simple choice about the things you buy, use and eat – and these are decisions that you would have to make anyway.

✦ Keep lists of your favourite meals and snacks so that you're never stuck for options in the early days (don't forget to keep plenty of them in the cupboard!).

✦ Don't feel that you've failed if you have a slip-up or two – it happens to all of us, and it doesn't mean that you're not a vegan any more. As long as you keep trying, you're still making a difference and doing a brilliant thing.

✦ Remind yourself that you're blazing a trail and living out your principles... and that is fantastic!

Community Support

Remember that you're part of an ever-growing, supportive group of people who are as passionate and excited as you are about veganism. Find your local community by visiting health food shops and fairs, and look out for vegan meet-ups and events. There is also an enormous and welcoming online community who will share their inspiration and wisdom with you at the touch of a button. Whatever vegan challenge you're pondering, there's someone out there who has been through the same thing. So if your housemate isn't up for another chat about aquafaba (see p.60), you can be sure that someone out there will be.

❦ ECO-LIVING

When you start to think about how the foods you buy are produced and sourced, you become aware of the way all your lifestyle choices affect the planet at large. You'll find yourself extending your ethical thinking into other areas of your life, and many vegans incorporate eco-friendly choices into as many aspects of their lifestyle as possible. For example, you could...

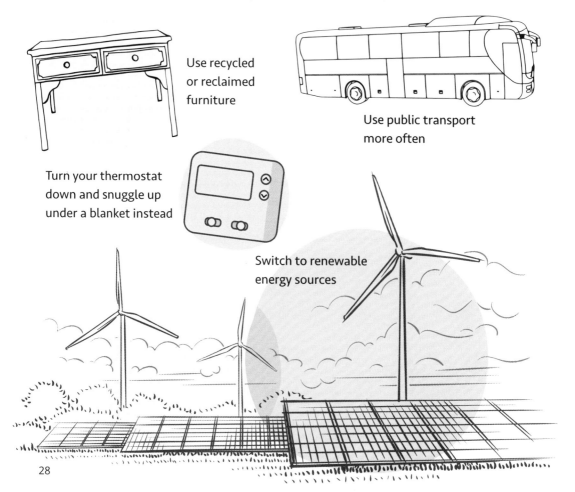

Use recycled or reclaimed furniture

Use public transport more often

Turn your thermostat down and snuggle up under a blanket instead

Switch to renewable energy sources

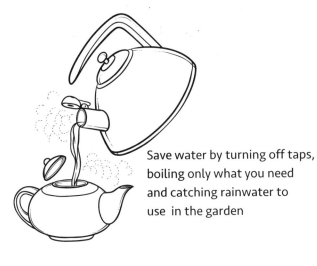

Save water by turning off taps, boiling only what you need and catching rainwater to use in the garden

Use natural cleaning products (or make your own, see p.85)

Compost your veggie leftovers and use that to grow your own produce

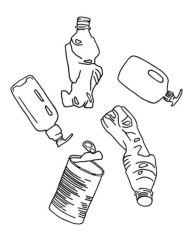

Ban the use of cleaning wipes and cotton buds in your household

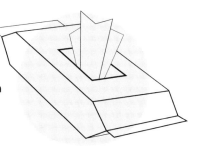

Avoid plastic packaging when shopping. Avoid using straws or plastic spoons when you're out and about (you can always carry eco-friendly versions in your bag)

CRUELTY-FREE ENTERTAINMENT

Sadly, it's not all about food and household products: animals are often exploited in the name of entertainment. Here are a few things you might want to avoid when veganising your leisure time – some are more obvious than others. And remember that if you want to take a more active role in ending this type of cruelty, there are often petitions online, peaceful protests and other forms of activism that you can consider joining.

What is it?	What does it involve?	What can you do?
Circus and animal shows	The number of circuses that still use animals is in decline but this type of 'entertainment' may still be found on trips abroad.	Boycott performances featuring animals and attend events where the entertainers are humans. You may want to avoid holiday providers who offer these trips as part of a package.
Zoos and aquaria	Zoos are businesses that make a profit by using animals to entertain visitors. Animals in captivity experience nothing like their natural environment and often display abnormal, stress-induced behaviours.	There is no educational value in watching bored creatures in unnatural surroundings. Watch nature documentaries instead or get to know your local wildlife by joining a conservation group.

Animals in advertising/ TV	Around 20 per cent of adverts use animals, and they also feature in TV programmes and films. Even a 'no animals were harmed' accreditation doesn't guarantee that these creatures were well cared for while not performing or living anything like a natural life.	Make a complaint to the relevant producers. You could also check out the Lion's Share initiative, which is supported by David Attenborough and raises funds to help endangered species.
Horse-drawn carriages and donkey rides	The use of horses to pull loads – including tourists – on busy polluted roads full of traffic and often in the heat.	If this takes place near you, it's worth contacting your local authority and putting pressure on for a ban. And take a rickshaw instead.
Cruel sports	Unfortunately, humans have come up with numerous ways of inflicting pain on their non-human friends, such as bullfighting and hunting.	This is an area where you might like to get active and make a stand – see the PETA website for links to current campaigns.
Paintballing	Paintballs are coated in glycerine and not vegan-friendly.	There are lots of alternatives for outdoor pursuits or team-building exercises! Try laser tag or have your work 'do' in an escape room instead!
Other areas	Dog shows, agility contests, live animal encounters, live nativity scenes, fishing...	There are some issues around humans' treatment of animals that are a real grey area. If these affect you or you want to give them more thought, the internet is a great place for further discussion and research.

CHAPTER TWO

THE VEGAN KITCHEN

Veganism opens up a world of exciting and nutritious new foods; you'll soon find yourself discovering ingredients you may have neglected before and trying out completely new options too. This chapter explains how to stock up your store cupboard with plant-based goodies, cook some decadent and delicious dishes, and get all the nutrients you need to flourish on your new eating regime.

WHAT'S ON THE MENU?

Your diet can include anything that is plant-based, and will be built around fruit, vegetables, legumes (beans and pulses), nuts, seeds and grains. From these basic building blocks you can make all sorts of meals (or buy them ready-made but, as with any diet, remember that pre-prepared products are processed, so use these in moderation – not all vegan foods are good for you!). You'll be spoilt for choice and soon find yourself wondering why this question ever crossed your mind. You can still eat curries, pasta, stir-fries, sandwiches, burgers, pizza, pies, bakes, decadent desserts and ice cream, as well as soups, salads and hearty stews. You may have not realised that some of the foods that you currently enjoy are vegan: beans on toast, spaghetti in tomato sauce, hummus and crackers, chips... You can still eat out, get take-away and travel abroad as a vegan.

When you first become vegan, do a little planning to make sure that you're getting all the nutrients you need and your new eating regime will soon be up and running. It isn't complicated – there are just a few rules to remember – but if you need an extra prompt, there are some good apps that help you to map your daily nutrition (see p.156).

Get Organised

The best way to enjoy a wide variety of vegan dishes is to prepare meals from scratch. They don't need to be complicated, but by cooking up your own recipes you can be certain of what's going into your food, use your favourite ingredients and save yourself some money. And you're much more likely to want to cook up tasty vegan treats if you get organised. Use your new eating regime as an excuse to declutter your kitchen, getting rid of any out-of-date items or non-vegan products that you want to phase out. (You could donate unwanted produce to a local food bank or give them to friends.) Go through the fridge, freezer and cupboards, and start with a blank slate.

In June 2016 two Swiss companies got together to bake a vegan cake that weighed over 430 kg. The record-breaking cake was then eaten by 3,000 lucky locals.

TO DO

+ Keep kitchen worktops clear

+ Buy a good supply of your core ingredients

+ Store the equipment and ingredients you'll use regularly in an easy-to-reach place

+ Plan food for the week ahead if you can, especially if you have any days when you'll be out and about

+ Have some standby go-to items ready in case you are running short on time

+ Pin up your favourite recipes on the kitchen noticeboard or keep a list of their ingredients on your phone

+ Invest in some reusable freezer bags or boxes for batch cooking

WHAT TO INCLUDE

Nuts and Seeds
One to two handfuls of these a day will help you to get the minerals and omega-3 fatty acids that you need to stay healthy. Sprinkle seeds on salads or soups, and remember that nut butters and milks are an option too.

Legumes
Include at least three portions of beans and pulses (or four if you're over 50), as these are a great source of protein. By incorporating just a portion (enough to fit in the palm of your hand) with every meal, you'll be well on the way to getting your daily needs covered. Tofu – which is made from soya beans – is a useful ingredient to add, as it is often fortified with calcium, too.

Grains and Starchy Veggies
Eat at least four portions a day and don't forget that wholemeal versions are best for you.

Fruit

Three portions a day: a wide variety is best. Many are rich in vitamin C, and don't forget to include some berries for their antioxidant powers.

Vegetables

At least five portions a day, which should include leafy greens such as kale, pak choi and broccoli, as they're great sources of calcium. Also, go for a range of different colours to maximise your vitamin intake.

And the Rest...

There are just a few extras that you need to include to fuel your body to the max.

Vitamin B12 – essential, but the one nutrient that you can't get from plants. Either take a B12 tablet daily or include B12-fortified foods, such as plant milk or fortified nutritional yeast, in your diet every day.

Iodine – found in veggies, but supplement that intake with the occasional shake of iodine salt on your meals. Alternatively, include nori sheets as a snack a couple of times a week.

Vitamin D – our bodies make this substance, which helps us to maintain healthy bones, when our skin is exposed to sunlight, so during less sunny months – if not year-round – it's important to take a supplement. Make sure that yours is vegan-friendly (see pp.136–137), since vitamin D2 is always derived from plants, but vitamin D3 can be derived from animal ingredients.

And don't forget to get enough **iron** – legumes, soya products, whole grains, leafy greens, and nuts and seeds are all great sources. Eat them alongside a good source of vitamin C so that your body can absorb all that goodness properly.

TIP:

Some companies manufacture an all-in-one vegan-friendly supplement that includes vitamin B12, iodine and vitamin D in one handy tablet.

STOCKING YOUR CUPBOARDS

Fill up your pantry with a few basics from each of these groups and you'll have everything you need for tasty vegan treats at your fingertips... just add the veggies!

Pickles
To enhance salads and sarnies

+ Capers
+ Chutney – mango is great with any veggie dish
+ Olives
+ Pickles (gherkins, jalapeños, onions, sauerkraut) – fermented veggies are so good for your gut
+ Sundried tomatoes

Grains and Flour (Wholemeal Where Possible)
Quality carbs to keep you energised

+ Couscous
+ Flour – include self-raising for baking
+ Oats
+ Pasta
+ Pearl barley – great to add to stews
+ Polenta
+ Quinoa
+ Rice

Seeds
Sprinkle on salads, soups and muesli or make into energy bars

+ Chia – best in smoothies and puddings (soak in plant-based milk before using)
+ Flax
+ Hemp
+ Pumpkin
+ Sunflower

Dried Fruit
For snacking, baking and making delicious desserts

+ Apricots
+ Cranberries
+ Dates
+ Figs
+ Raisins

Canned and Dried Pulses
To make hearty and wholesome meals

+ Beans – all types
+ Lentils
+ Chickpeas

Nuts

Nutrient-rich but take care to stick to just one or two handfuls a day

- Almonds
- Brazil nuts – eat two a day for selenium
- Cashews – a great addition to stir-fries
- Nut butters
- Peanuts
- Pistachios
- Walnuts

Condiments

Spice up your meals

- Brown sauce
- Ketchup
- Vegan mayo
- Mustard
- Vegan pesto
- Oils – flax, olive and vegetable all have health benefits when used in moderation
- Soy sauce
- Sweet chilli sauce (hide some in your bag if you're eating out and sense a bland-salad moment coming on!)
- Tahini
- Vinegars (balsamic, red wine and rice vinegar)

Herbs, Seasonings and Spices

Build up a collection as you explore vegan cooking and discover your favourite dishes. Spices are handy store-cupboard staples but can be pricey, so pick a few that you really enjoy, rather than buying up the whole shelf. You can choose dried herbs or fresh ones – or even grow your own, so you'll always have your favourites to hand.

- Basil
- Chilli powder
- Cinnamon
- Cumin
- Garlic powder
- Kala namak (black salt with an eggy flavour)
- Nutmeg
- Nutritional yeast – an essential, which gives a lovely cheesy flavour to dishes
- Oregano
- Paprika
- Peppercorns
- Sea salt – a good source of iodine
- Turmeric – a superfood with anti-inflammatory properties

QUALITY CALCIUM

Along with protein (see pp.66–67), one of the most important things to consider when you switch to a vegan diet is where you'll get your calcium from. Leafy greens, broccoli, dried figs and chia seeds are great sources, as well as many fortified plant milks and yogurts (just two cups of these a day will fulfil two-thirds of your requirements). You can also buy calcium-set tofu – a 100 g portion of this contains 50 per cent of your daily calcium needs. So aim to eat three of these foodstuffs a day and you should have it covered.

Easy Calcium Hits

- Make a smoothie with your favourite fruit and calcium-fortified plant milk.

- Throw some extra veggies into your stir-fry or sauce – or just cook a portion of broccoli to have on the side.

- Make up some trail mix and have a handful as a snack.

- Scramble some tofu for breakfast (see pp.76) for a speedy calcium-rich start to the day.

- Make a coffee or hot chocolate with your favourite nut-based milk.

PLANT MILKS

There's such a wide range of plant-based milks available that you're spoilt for choice and – since they contain no cholesterol or dairy nasties – they're usually much better for you too. (Just watch out for those that are sweetened and may have added sugars.) Here's an at-a-glance guide to the different options you can find on the supermarket shelves.

Type of Milk	Description	Try it
Almond milk	Thick and full of nutrients	In coffee or on cereal
Coconut milk	Thick and creamy	In cakes or for ice cream. Refrigerate overnight and whip to substitute for whipped cream
Hazelnut milk	Thin, with a lovely nutty flavour	In coffee or for sipping
Hemp milk	Creamy and super nutritious – high in calcium, omega fats and protein	In baking – but best in savoury dishes, as it has a strong flavour
Flax milk	Thin and smooth	For drinking, or to make pancakes or muffins
Oat milk	Thick with a sweet taste	For drinking, baking cookies or adding to soups
Rice milk	Watery texture with a plain, sweet taste	On cereal or in desserts, but you'll need to thicken it for baking
Soya milk	Creamy, and high in protein and unsaturated fats	To drink or in any recipe which lists dairy

Make Your Own Nut Milk

Nut milks are incredibly versatile and have a wonderful flavour. By learning to make your own, you can sweeten to taste and always make sure you have a fresh supply. Try experimenting with different nuts – the method is the same – but be sure to choose raw, unsalted ones as your starting point (and avoid skins, if possible).

Makes 500 ml

- 250 g raw nuts
- 500 ml water, plus more for soaking
- Maple syrup or agave syrup, to taste

Method

1. Soak the nuts in water (either overnight, at room temperature, or in the fridge for up to 48 hours). The longer you soak them, the creamier your milk will be.

2. Drain the nuts, rinse them and place in a blender. Add 500 ml of fresh water and a little syrup (if using). Blitz for 3 minutes or so, until smooth.

3. Sieve the mixture through a muslin cloth into a bowl (or use a clean, open-weave tea towel), making sure to squeeze out every drop. Store the milk in a sealed container in the fridge for up to 3 days.

TIP:

For thinner milk, add a little more water to the blender before processing. If you prefer it thicker, add a little less.

 # LABEL LOOKOUT

Once you become vegan, you'll often find yourself peering at food labels and puzzling out the ingredients. Some things to avoid are obvious – such as milk powder and eggs – but others might have misleading names or mystery components. Here's what to look out for when you're picking a new product.

The Most Common Offenders

- Albumin – a binder derived from eggs
- Casein – protein from milk
- Gelatine – animal-derived thickeners (use agar-agar instead)

- Lactose – a milk sugar
- Whey – derived from milk

Other Ingredients to Avoid

Aspic – a thickener derived from animal products and gelatine

Carmine (cochineal) – red colouring made from crushed beetles

Castoreum – flavouring taken from beavers' scent glands

Cod liver oil – often found in supplements, and (obviously) taken from fish

Collagen – derived from the skin, connective tissues and bones of cows, chickens, pigs, fish...

Elastin – taken from the ligaments and blood vessels of cattle

Fish sauce – made from oysters, shrimp or fermented fish

Honey – essential to the health of a beehive... non-essential to humans!

Isinglass – made from fish bladders and often used in beer-making

Keratin – derived from the skin, connective tissues and bones of cows, chickens, pigs, fish

L-cysteine – made from animal fur and feathers

Lard – animal fat

Omega-3 fatty acids – if something is enriched with omega-3s, it may well have come from fish

Pepsin – a clotting agent taken from pigs' stomachs

Propolis – made by bees when building hives

Rennet – taken from the stomachs of newly born calves

Royal jelly – secreted by bees

Shellac – insect secretion used to glaze food and sweets

Shortening – traditionally contains lard, unless labelled 'vegetable-based'

Suet – fat taken from the kidneys of cows and sheep

Tallow – animal fat

Vitamin D3 – usually derived from fish oil or lanolin

Know your Numbers

Some additives (particularly colourings) are derived from animals, so have this checklist to hand – you could keep a photo on your phone – when you're scrutinising your E-numbers:

E120 – carmine

E322 – lecithin*

E422 – glycerol*

E441 – gelatine

E471 – fatty acids*

E542 – bone phosphate (ground-up bones used to moisten food)

E631 – disodium inosinate*

E901 – beeswax

E904 – shellac

E910 – L-cysteine

E913 – lanolin (secreted by sheep)

E920 – derived from L-cysteine

E921 – derived from L-cysteine

E966 – lactitol (a sweetener made from lactose)

*These additives may come from a plant- or animal-based source. Check the manufacturer's website for more information or look for one of the vegan trademarks.

And Finally

Here's just one more list of what to look out for when you're shopping. These are products that you might assume to be vegan (and, indeed, sometimes they are) but occasionally they can have a sneaky ingredient in them to catch you out, so double-check them.

Beer and wine – ingredients lists won't help here, so see pp.62–63 for vegan options

Bread – could contain milk, butter or eggs

Dark chocolate – it's not always dairy-free

Fizzy drinks – can contain animal-derived colourings (especially red or orange drinks)

Fruit juice – check additives, if fortified

Roast nuts – can contain gelatine

Sugar – in the US especially this can be processed through bone fragments

Worcestershire sauce – usually contains anchovies

IT'S NOT COMPLICATED!

It may seem that there's a lot to look out for when shopping, but don't worry: you'll soon work out which products are vegan-friendly and get to grips with checking out labels. An internet search for 'accidentally vegan' is a good way of finding lists of everyday products that contain no animal-based ingredients. There are likely to be many things that you haven't even realised are vegan, which you already eat regularly!

Label Lookout

If a product carries the Vegan Society's sunflower logo or the V-Label (or the Certified Vegan Logo in the US), it is definitely vegan. Other vegan labelling is voluntary (and carried out according to the manufacturer's definition of the term), but should be absolutely fine.

Some labels that don't necessarily mean your product is vegan include:

+ Dairy-free

+ Free from

+ Natural ingredients

+ Organic

Take care if products are marked 'enriched', or mention added vitamins or omega-3, for example, as these may have come from animal sources.

Is it Vegan?

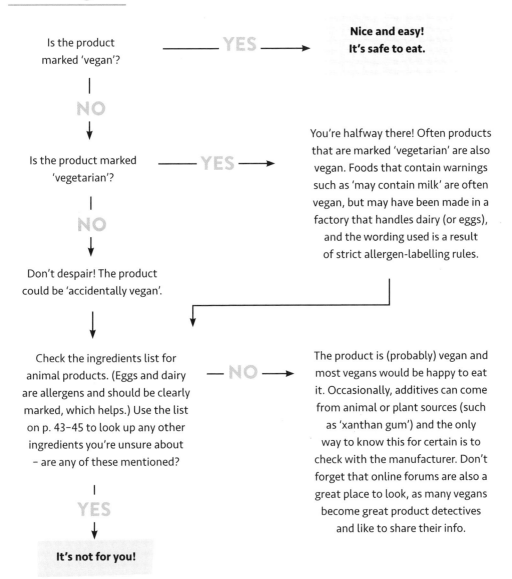

Is the product marked 'vegan'? —————— YES ——————→ **Nice and easy! It's safe to eat.**

NO

Is the product marked 'vegetarian'? ——— YES ——→ You're halfway there! Often products that are marked 'vegetarian' are also vegan. Foods that contain warnings such as 'may contain milk' are often vegan, but may have been made in a factory that handles dairy (or eggs), and the wording used is a result of strict allergen-labelling rules.

NO

Don't despair! The product could be 'accidentally vegan'.

Check the ingredients list for animal products. (Eggs and dairy are allergens and should be clearly marked, which helps.) Use the list on p. 43–45 to look up any other ingredients you're unsure about – are any of these mentioned? — NO —→ The product is (probably) vegan and most vegans would be happy to eat it. Occasionally, additives can come from animal or plant sources (such as 'xanthan gum') and the only way to know this for certain is to check with the manufacturer. Don't forget that online forums are also a great place to look, as many vegans become great product detectives and like to share their info.

YES

It's not for you!

BRILLIANT BREAKFASTS

Don't be tempted to just grab a banana on the way out of the house, when there are so many ways to start the day with a hearty, healthy vegan breakfast. This is your opportunity to get a protein boost first thing in the morning, and if you combine that with some carbs, you'll fill yourself up with some slow-burning energy to keep you going until lunch. Using nut milk, and topping your breakfasts with chopped nuts and seeds, is a good start. You could also add vegan protein powder to any of the milk-based recipes. (Each makes one serving unless otherwise stated.)

Chocolate Chia Pot

Prepare this the night before and it will set in the fridge, ready for the morning. Just add 250 ml of plant milk (almond, soya and coconut work best) to a bowl or lidded pot (if you want to take your breakfast to work with you) and stir in 3 tbsp chia seeds and 1½ tbsp cocoa powder. Sweeten with a little maple syrup or ½ tsp vanilla extract. In the morning top with your choice of fresh berries, chopped nuts or cocoa nibs.

Vegan Pancakes
(makes 12 pancakes)

Mix together 150 g plain flour, 2 tbsp baking powder and a pinch of salt. Then stir in 300 ml soya or almond milk, 1 tbsp oil and 2 tbsp maple syrup. Mix thoroughly and rest your batter in the fridge, if you have time. Heat some oil in a heavy-based frying pan and drop your mixture in, a ladleful at a time. Flip each pancake and cook until lightly browned on both sides. Serve with fruit, chopped nuts a spoonful of jam or a drizzle of maple syrup.

Overnight Oats

Make up a jar of oats to enjoy in the morning, by taking 45 g rolled oats and adding any of these winning combinations: 125 ml of your favourite plant milk, half a banana (mashed), ¼ tsp cinnamon, ¼ tsp nutmeg OR 125 ml coffee, 2 tsp cocoa powder and a chopped date OR 2 tbsp peanut butter and 1 tbsp maple syrup. Stir your ingredients and leave covered in the fridge overnight. When you get up, sprinkle with dried fruit and chopped nuts or seeds.

Super-speedy Options

If toast's your thing, why not add any of these to your morning slice: smashed avocado, hummus, salsa, baked beans, mushrooms, spinach... Or whip up a smoothie with 250 ml plant milk, a banana, a handful of berries and a splash of OJ.

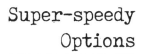

SAVOURY SPINACH SOUFFLÉS

These are easy to make and very tasty too, so if you fancy a savoury breakfast treat, get the food processor out and you'll have these ready to go in the oven in just 10 minutes.

Makes 2

A little olive oil

15 g spinach, roughly chopped

300 g silken tofu

4 tbsp chickpea flour

3 tbsp nutritional yeast

1 tsp baking powder

1 clove garlic

Salt and pepper

1. Preheat the oven to 180°C and grease two ramekin dishes.

2. Sauté the spinach in the oil until wilted. Divide it between the two ramekins.

3. Put the tofu, flour, nutritional yeast, baking powder and garlic in a food processor, and blitz until smooth. Season and then pour over the spinach mixture, leaving room at the top of your ramekin for the soufflés to puff up.

4. Bake for 45 minutes and serve hot.

TIP:

You can use any combination of veggies you like, so have fun experimenting. Courgettes, spring onions, mushrooms and kale are all good options.

THE THRIFTY VEGAN

Eating a vegan diet doesn't need to break the bank. There are some wonderful ready-made vegan products on the shelves – which are great for treats or when you're pushed for time – but they can be expensive. Cooking from scratch is the way to go if you want to save some pennies, and there's plenty you can do to cut back on expense and waste in the kitchen.

Bulk-buy dry goods, such as rice, nuts, pasta, pulses and seeds, and look out for multibuy deals at your local health food store. You can get dry beans too; they need to be soaked and then boiled for a little longer, but doing this is much cheaper than buying them canned. (Cook up a big batch, then cool and freeze the beans to use later.)

Shop seasonally – when your meals are based around fruits and veggies, you can make the most of whatever is in season at the time. These ingredients will be cheaper and taste better, too.

If a recipe calls for half a marrow or aubergine, for example, **chop the whole thing** and keep the extra portion in the fridge to throw into a stir-fry (rather than throwing it into the bin). You could even grill these bits while you're cooking, cool them and add to salads or wraps the next day.

Visit your nearest **Chinese supermarket** to pick up bargain tofu, noodles, miso paste, tinned jackfruit and dried sweet potato... plus lots of other vegan treats.

Get creative and find ways to **use up your odds and ends**, rather than leaving them languishing in the fridge. Make it your mission to leave no ingredient behind! Overripe bananas make great banana bread, for example, or herbs can be made into tea or fried in non-dairy butter and drizzled over pasta. (Check online for lots of cunning ideas along these lines.)

Grow your own! Nothing tastes better than freshly cut beans or peppers from your garden. You don't need to have lots of space to produce your own ingredients: tomatoes and potatoes can be grown in pots, and your windowsill is the perfect place for a mini herb garden. (In fact, growing your own fresh herbs and salad leaves is a great money-saver.)

Plan ahead – if you can work out your meals for the week ahead and get the ingredients in, you're much less likely to end up buying pricey last-minute meals or searching for vegan takeaway options!

Use your freezer! Cook up an extra portion (or two) of your latest soup or stew and freeze for another day. Freeze herbs in ice-cube trays to add to stocks or teas: pour fresh water into the tray to about a quarter full, then add your chopped herbs and top up with more water. And don't forget that shop-bought frozen veggies, fruit and berries are often cheaper than fresh ones, and great to throw into soups, stews and smoothies.

Make your own nut and plant milks (see p.41)

Warming Butternut Squash Soup

This recipe is simple but packed full of flavour, showing just how tasty plant-based food can be. It's decadent and delicious: a great one for impressing your non-vegan friends.

Serves 4 as a starter, or 2 as a main

1 butternut squash

1 x 200 g carton of coconut cream

½ tsp turmeric

½ tsp cumin

Salt and pepper

A sprig of parsley, slices of apple or
a swirl of vegan cream (optional)

You can season the seeds and roast them covered in a little olive oil or fry them with some soy sauce. Use to snack on or garnish the soup?

1. Peel the squash, removing the seeds, and cut it into small chunks.

2. Place in a saucepan and (just) cover with water. Boil for 10 minutes or until soft.

3. Add the spices and the coconut cream, keeping the remaining cooking water in the pan to form the base for your soup. Heat gently until the coconut cream melts, stirring occasionally.

4. Use a stick blender to whizz the soup to your desired consistency, then add salt and pepper to taste.

5. Garnish with a sprig of parsley, slices of apple or a swirl of vegan cream and serve with crusty bread.

Turmeric is a superfood that the body absorbs best when combined with pepper and cumin, so this recipe boosts your body as well as your spirits!

 # VEGAN SNACKS

Snacking can be the best way to keep you on track when you're first starting your vegan journey. Take some nibbles with you when you're out and about so you're never stuck for something to eat, and have a few stashed away at home. Here are some easy options for speedy plant-based eats:

♦ Crackers and nut butter

♦ Crisps – look for baked varieties or try veggie crisps for a change

♦ Hummus and veggie sticks – chop some when you're prepping your evening meal

♦ Fruit laces – buy or make your own

♦ Fruit – try something new or exotic

- Popped corn or lotus seeds

- Rice cakes topped with smashed avocado and a squeeze of lemon

- Roasted chickpeas – just toss them straight out of the can in a little oil, season and pop in the oven for 20 minutes

- Tortilla chips and salsa

- Trail mix – prepare your own, with your favourite combo of nuts, seeds and dried fruit

CHOC-AND-DATE BITES

These bite-sized treats are brilliant for when you need a quick burst of energy. They're naturally sweetened and the nuts pack a protein punch, too. These will store in the fridge for up to a week – if you can resist them for that long!

Makes 10 balls

8 dates

60 g mixed nuts

50 g desiccated coconut

1 tbsp cocoa powder

½ tsp cinnamon

A pinch of ginger (optional)

1. Roughly chop the dates and add to the blender with the nuts, coconut, cocoa powder, cinnamon and ginger.

2. Pulse until the dates and nuts are broken up, and the mixture binds together.

3. Roll the mixture into balls, a tablespoon at a time, and enjoy.

HOW TO VEGANISE A RECIPE

There are a million vegan recipes online, but if you spot something which isn't and still takes your fancy, you can always veganise it with a few simple swaps. Here's how:

Item to be Replaced	Replace With
Butter	Vegan spread or olive oil
Buttermilk	250 ml soya milk + 1 tsp lemon juice (let the mixture separate)
Condensed milk	Canned coconut milk
Double cream	Refrigerate a can of coconut milk for 48 hours and use the top layer
Gelatine	Agar-agar
Honey	Maple, agave or golden syrup
Milk	Soya milk is good for baking (or see p. 41)

Fake One Egg...

Each of these swaps will replace one egg in cooking.

TO BIND (sweet recipes):

3 tbsp apple puree
or ½ banana, mashed
or 3 tbsp peanut butter
or 3 tbsp chickpea flour +
3 tbsp water

TO BIND (any recipes):

1 tbsp flaxseeds + 3 tbsp water
or 1 tbsp chia seeds stirred into
3 tbsp water and left to rest
or 2 tbsp cornflour + 2 tbsp
water
or 60 g plain soya yogurt

FOR RAISING:

Bicarbonate of soda +
warm water
or 1 tsp baking soda + 2 tsp
lemon juice

TO REPLACE AN EGG WHITE:

2 tbsp aquafaba (use 3 tbsp to
replace a whole egg)
or 1 tsp agar-agar + 1 tbsp
water (add to water, rest for
5 minutes and then warm
gently in a pan to dissolve)

AQUAFABA

This wonder-ingredient has made all sorts of recipes a possibility on a plant-based diet, as it can replace egg whites when baking, so meringues are back on the menu. It's actually chickpea water, and you can buy it in cans, get it by draining the liquid from a can of chickpeas or – if you're cooking up dry beans you can make your own. Once the beans have boiled, pour the cooking water into ice-cube trays and freeze; store the cubes in freezer bags and defrost when you're ready to whip up some meringues.

For an easy vegan mayo, just take 3 tbsp aquafaba (or defrost 3 cubes), and blend with 120 ml oil, a squeeze of lemon juice and seasoning. You can add chopped herbs or garlic, too.

Meringue Nests with Strawberries and Cream

Makes about 12 large or 25 small nests

The liquid from 1 x 400 g can chickpeas

100 g golden caster sugar

To serve:

Dark chocolate

Soya cream

Fresh berries

1. Heat the oven to 90°C and line a baking tray with parchment.

2. Whisk the chickpea water into soft peaks using an electric whisk. (This may take longer than you expect.)

3. Add the caster sugar a little at a time, while whisking, until the mixture becomes thick and shiny.

4. Spoon blobs of mixture on to your baking tray (or pipe them if you're feeling artistic) and bake in the oven until crisp. This will take about 1 hour 15 minutes.

5. Drizzle with melted dark chocolate (if liked), and top with soya cream and fresh berries.

TIP:

For a decadent-looking dessert why not turn your meringues into an Eton mess? This quantity will serve 4: break up your meringues and mix together with soya cream and chopped strawberries. Spoon into glasses and serve chilled.

☿ TIME FOR A TIPPLE

At first glance the world of vegan-friendly alcohol can seem a bit of a mystery, as manufacturers aren't obliged to list the ingredients on most drinks, and animal products can be used in the production process. But with a little research – and the help of these handy tips – you can make sure that you always know the best option for a cruelty-free drink.

Wine

Manufacturers may use animal-derived products to filter out impurities in wines: egg and dairy protein are often used for reds, while isinglass – derived from fish guts – is used for whites, rosés and sparkling varieties. Look out for the label 'not filtered' as an indication that the wines are vegan-friendly and bear in mind that most supermarkets sell an own-brand vegan wine. For more information, the Barnivore website has a great searchable database to help you choose.

Beers

If you stick to mainstream, vegan-friendly brands, you can avoid products that have been filtered through isinglass – a process that is still used in producing most real ales. So don't order draft ales; instead go for Becks, Bud, Bulmers, Cobra, Corona, Carlsberg, Heineken, Peroni, San Miguel or Stella, which are all vegan. You can also check your favourite brew online, or opt for Belgian or German beers, since strict brewing laws in these countries mean that no animal derivatives are used in their production.

Ciders

Most ciders are refined using animal products and are not vegan friendly. Your best option here is to do a little online research to find a local producer who can confirm their production methods.

Spirits

Cream-based liquors are obvious no-nos, and some cocktails use dairy or egg in their ingredients, but you should be able to identify these from the bar menu. Watch out for Worcestershire sauce in Bloody Marys and tomato-juice mixes. Vegan-friendly brands include: Bacardi, Jack Daniel's, Jägermeister, Pimm's and Smirnoff.

Soft Drinks and Mixers

Avoid red or orange soda drinks, which may use cochineal (or other animal derivatives) as a colourant. Red Bull, Coca-Cola and Schweppes products are all vegan and a safe bet. Another thing to watch out for is concentrated fruit juice, which may have been distilled using non-vegan products.

CHOC CHIP COOKIES

Who'd have thought it – cookies made from pulses? These tasty treats give you all the proteiny goodness of chickpeas and will satisfy your craving for something sweet at the same time.

Makes 6 large cookies

1 x 400 g can chickpeas, drained and rinsed

2 tbsp peanut butter

1 tbsp maple syrup

2 tsp vanilla extract

1 tsp baking powder

75 g cocoa nibs or chocolate chips

1. Preheat the oven to 180°C and grease a baking tray (or line a silicon mat with baking parchment).

2. Blitz the chickpeas in a blender until smooth; then add in the peanut butter, maple syrup, vanilla extract and baking powder. Blend again until smooth and creamy.

3. Stir through the cocoa nibs or chocolate chips.

4. Divide the dough into 6 pieces, roll into balls and then press them down gently on the baking tray.

5. Bake for 15 minutes, until golden. Remove from the oven and rest for 5 minutes. Move to a wire rack to cool and see how long you can wait before trying one!

These taste lovely served warm with a little coconut ice-cream. You can even eat the cookie mixture without cooking it – no eggs, so no need to worry – but if you're doing this, leave out the baking powder and chill the dough in the fridge first.

Packing in the Protein

It's a myth that eating meat and dairy products is the
best way of getting protein in our diets. Plants are excellent
sources of it and a much better food to consume, as they come
with lots of bonus nutrients and absolutely no cholesterol.

When you first go vegan, you may be wondering how much protein
you need; there are online calculators that will help you to work this out,
based on your body weight, but a good rule of thumb is to incorporate
a source of plant protein at every meal, including breakfast.

As an example, the average recommended protein requirement for a woman
is 46 g and for a man 56 g – as you can see from the table opposite, by
including a good source of protein at every meal, it's not too hard to
achieve your goal. (Remember, though, that the amount of protein you
need will vary according to your weight, age and activity level.)

Many top athletes are vegan, proving just how nutritious a plant-based
diet can be. They include record-breaking ultrarunner Scott Jurek,
pro surfer Tia Blanco, Olympic rower David Smith, and top
tennis Grand Slammers Venus and Serena Williams.

Top Protein Sources

Food	Amount of protein (per average serving)
Almonds	6 g (per 30 g – a small handful)
Avocado	2 g (per ¼ avocado)
Black beans; butter beans	8 g (per 85 g)
Boiled chickpeas; boiled lentils	9 g (per 100 g)
Boiled peas	5 g (per 100 g)
Broccoli	3 g (per 80 g, cooked)
Chia seeds	4 g (per 30 g)
Edamame	16 g (per 85 g)
Nutritional yeast	9 g (per 30 g or 2 tbsp)
Peanuts/peanut butter	7 g (per 30 g – a small handful – or 2 tbsp)
Pumpkin seeds	5 g (per 30 g)
Quinoa; wild rice	8 g (per 200 g)
Seitan (see p.74)	33 g (per 100 g)
Spinach	4 g (per 100 g)
Tempeh	19 g (per 100 g)
Tofu	12 g (per 85 g)
Wholemeal bread	4 g (per slice)

Note: Nuts and seeds are a great source of protein, but don't forget that they have a high fat content, so stick to a handful or two of them a day.

Three-bean Chilli

Slow-cooker meals are great to dip into, especially if you live with others who want to eat at different times. This three-bean chilli is so easy to prepare and it includes plenty of protein-rich pulses in the mix. Why not make a double portion and freeze the extra for another day?

Serves 4

1 tbsp olive oil

1 onion, finely chopped

Salt and pepper

1 red chilli, finely chopped

1 tsp coriander seeds

1 tsp cumin

3 garlic cloves, crushed

1 red pepper, chopped

3 carrots, sliced

Punnet mushrooms

1 star anise

1 tbsp white wine vinegar

1 x 400 g can kidney beans

1 x 400 g can black beans

1 x 400 g can cannellini beans

1 x 400 g can chopped tomatoes

450 ml stock

If you don't have a slow cooker, prepare this on the hob. Use 600 ml stock and cook for 40 minutes over a low heat, stirring and adding a little water when needed.

1. Switch on the slow cooker. Heat the oil in a large pan and gently cook the onion for 3–4 minutes, until soft. Season, and then stir in the chilli, coriander seeds and garlic, and cook for a few minutes more.

2. Add the pepper, carrots and star anise, and turn down the heat. Cook for 15 minutes, stirring occasionally; then add the vinegar, beans, tomatoes and a splash of the stock. Simmer for a few minutes.

3. Transfer to the slow cooker and add the remaining stock. Cover and cook for 8 hours on a low setting. Remove the star anise before serving with tortillas, lime and vegan sour cream.

Make your own sour cream by whizzing up 150 g cashews with a couple of tablespoons of lime juice and 2 tsp nutritional yeast.

MASON-JAR MAGIC

Mason-jar lunches are great for a tasty, easily grabbable meal on the go. Whether you want to take something sweet or savoury – cold or hot – you can come up with a combination that suits you.

Tasty Salads

Layer up hummus, any veggies you fancy (cherry tomatoes, chopped peppers, carrot or courgette ribbons, sweetcorn, olives, celery, bean sprouts…) and your favourite salad leaves (pop them in last so that they won't wilt at the bottom of the jar). You can add cooked rice, couscous or quinoa, or take some sliced pitta bread as an accompaniment. And don't forget to bring along a little tub of your favourite home-made vinaigrette or dressing to pour on before you eat.

TIP:

Reuse little plastic dessert tubs by balancing them at the top of your jar, before screwing on the lid, to transport dressings or dips.

Noodle Soup

Pop some parboiled ramen noodles into the base of your jar, followed by soy sauce, miso paste and/or chilli sauce, and then top with chopped veggies (spring onions, carrot strips, edamame beans and sliced mushrooms work well). Just add hot water when you're ready to eat for a tasty noodle soup.

TIP:

These will keep in the fridge for 2–3 days, so you can make up a few at a time.

Sweet Treats

For a lunchtime dessert, pile chopped banana or other fruit into your jar, and make a 'dip' of nut butter and choc chips, or vegan cream flavoured with a little cinnamon. Alternatively, try a base layer of soya yogurt topped with berries and some crunchy nuts and seeds, with a little maple syrup to drizzle across the top.

 # SPEEDY SANDWICHES

If you think that your sandwiches are going to be hummus-based for evermore, think again. Here are just a few of the combinations you can try, but you'll soon come up with your own favourites – don't forget that the leftovers from last night's supper could taste amazing sandwiched between two slices of bread and garnished with a little mango chutney or mustard.

Sautéed mushroom, yellow pepper and garlic on crusty bread with vegan mayo

Vegan cheese, sliced avocado and tomato

Choc-nut spread with sliced fruit

Tomatoes, basil and olives

Vegan cream cheese with chopped dates and walnuts

Vegan cottage cheese, agave syrup, berries and flaked almonds

Leftover roast veggies, hummus and tomato puree

Scrambled tofu (see p.76), cress and chopped cherry tomatoes

Peanut butter and jam

Mixed salad, hummus, sundried tomatoes and home-made pesto (see p.77)

Fake bacon, lettuce, tomatoes and vegan mayo

Yeast extract, vegan cream cheese and sliced cucumber

Vegan cheese, mango chutney, crispy lettuce and beef tomatoes

MEAT SWAPS

If you're new to plant-based eating, you might be surprised when you start to explore the world of meat alternatives. There are dozens of products that you can use to replace animal protein in your favourite meals and snacks, including fake meat products – and many of them are very similar to the food they're imitating. If these appeal to you, give them a try, but don't forget that they are processed and should not be a daily choice. So what about the other alternatives to using meat in your meals? Here's a quick guide to what's out there and how you can use it.

Food	What is it?	What do I do with it?
Jackfruit	A tropical fruit that is a great substitute for pulled pork or chicken. Use in wraps, tacos, burritos, on top of pizzas, or in chillies, curries and sweet-and-sour sauces.	Buy tinned jackfruit (in brine is best), rinse and slice. Then simmer in water for 20 minutes and break it up to use in burritos. Alternatively, add to your cooking sauce and simmer for 20 minutes.
Mushrooms	Mushrooms have a great texture and lots of flavour, if you buy them fresh, and are good for you although not high in protein, so pick a protein-rich side dish.	Pick portobello mushrooms – season and barbecue – to stand in for burger patties or add chunky pieces to a curry sauce. Roast small slices on a baking sheet for an hour, doused in olive oil, garlic and rosemary; they will resemble crispy bacon bits.
Seitan	Seitan is concentrated wheat gluten and is packed with protein. It is versatile and will take on the flavours you're using in your recipe (or it can be marinated).	Use in stir-fries alongside your favourite sauce – black bean works well – or coat in breadcrumbs and bake for fake chicken nuggets.

Tempeh	Like tofu, tempeh is soya-based, but it's also fermented (which benefits your gut).	Buy pre-marinated to save time. Simply slice, stir-fry it with seasoning and serve with chilli sauce – or use in sweet-and-sour sauces or as an alternative in sandwich fillings.
Tofu	Made from soya beans, there are three types of tofu. Both 'Firm' and 'Extra firm' need pressing before use, to remove moisture, and then marinating. 'Silken' tofu can be used straight from the pack and is best for blending or crumbling, as it's so soft.	For a simple marinade: add 2 tbsp soy sauce, 1 tbsp cider vinegar, 1 tbsp maple syrup, 1 tsp cornflour and 1 tsp garlic powder. (Marinate for at least 2 hours before cooking.) If you're making dessert, be sure to use enough sweet ingredients to mask tofu's savoury taste.
TVP	Textured Vegetable Protein is made from dried soya powder and needs to be rehydrated before use.	Just mix with veggie stock and use in stews, stir-fries and Bolognese sauce or to make burgers... TVP makes nice meatballs to go with pasta, too.

If you really miss bacon, use sliced tempeh or thinly sliced aubergine instead. Brush the slices with a mixture of olive oil, soy sauce, maple syrup, and a pinch of smoked paprika and black pepper, before baking for 45 minutes on each side at 120°C. And – strange but true – some bacon-flavoured crisps and snacks are vegan-friendly, so check out the snack aisle if you crave the taste.

SCRAMBLED TOFU

This speedy recipe is a vegan version of scrambled eggs. It's also a great way to include tofu in your day without any need for marinating it first. Whip some up for a nutritious breakfast at the weekend or have it as a super-easy TV supper.

Serves 1

1–2 tbsp olive oil

1 block of tofu, pressed

2 tbsp nutritional yeast

½ tsp garlic powder

¼ tsp onion powder

½ tsp paprika

Salt and pepper to taste

Cherry tomatoes, chives or chopped avocado (optional)

1. Cut the tofu into pieces and then mash with a fork, leaving a few bigger chunks.

2. Heat the oil in a frying pan, add the tofu and sauté gently.

3. Add in the nutritional yeast, the garlic powder, the onion powder and the paprika. Stir and cook for 5–10 minutes.

4. Season and serve on toast with some sautéed cherry tomatoes, chives or chopped avocado.

TIP:

Use black salt (kala namak) to give your scramble an eggy flavour.

NUTRITIONAL YEAST

Unlike traditional yeast, which is used as a raising agent in food, deactivated nutritional yeast has a wonderful cheesy flavour, and is a great addition to savoury sauces and bakes. 'Nooch' is also high in fibre and rich in vitamins, with some versions providing almost all of the RDA for vitamin B12, so it's a valuable addition to your daily diet.

Use nutritional yeast to blend up a batch of vegan pesto, which you can add to sandwiches, salads or pasta, or use as a tasty dip. Just whizz: 140 g fresh basil leaves, 3 tbsp pine nuts (or walnuts), 2 cloves of garlic and at least 2 tbsp nutritional yeast (to taste) in a blender to form a paste. Then blend in 3 tbsp olive oil followed by 4 tbsp water, each a tablespoon at a time. Season with salt and pepper, and your pesto is ready!

VEGGIE BOWL BONANZA

Veggie bowls are so quick and easy to put together – and a great way of including all your food groups in one hit. With so many possible combinations of ingredients, you can make every meal a little different and mix up the various elements to find your favourite. Pick an item – or two! – from each column below and combine them to make a veggie bowl bursting with flavour.

Build Your Own Veggie Bowl

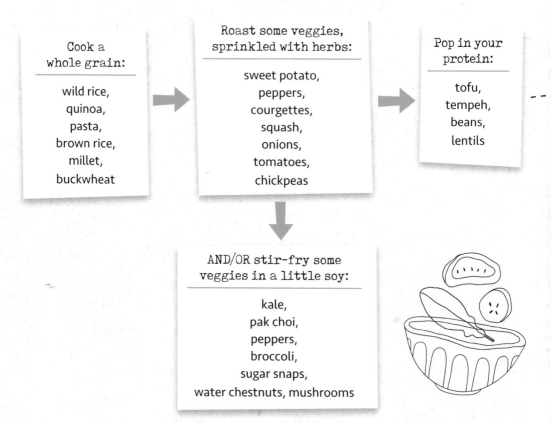

Cook a
whole grain:

wild rice,
quinoa,
pasta,
brown rice,
millet,
buckwheat

Roast some veggies,
sprinkled with herbs:

sweet potato,
peppers,
courgettes,
squash,
onions,
tomatoes,
chickpeas

Pop in your
protein:

tofu,
tempeh,
beans,
lentils

AND/OR stir-fry some
veggies in a little soy:

kale,
pak choi,
peppers,
broccoli,
sugar snaps,
water chestnuts, mushrooms

TIP:

For perfect roast veggies, chop evenly, drizzle with
a tablespoon or two of olive oil, and sprinkle with
mixed dried herbs and some chopped garlic.
Roast for 40 minutes at 180°C, turning occasionally.

Don't forget that you can pre-cook roast veggies or grains at the start of
the week to save time when assembling your veggie bowl. Also remember
to take care with cooked rice: it must be cooled and refrigerated as soon as
possible, and then reheated thoroughly, or it can make you unwell.

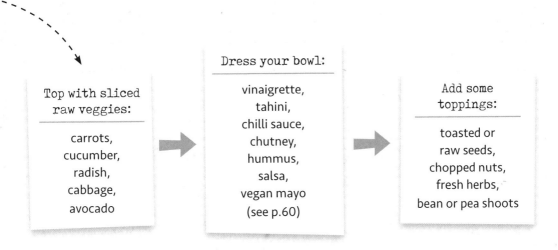

**Top with sliced
raw veggies:**

carrots,
cucumber,
radish,
cabbage,
avocado

Dress your bowl:

vinaigrette,
tahini,
chilli sauce,
chutney,
hummus,
salsa,
vegan mayo
(see p.60)

**Add some
toppings:**

toasted or
raw seeds,
chopped nuts,
fresh herbs,
bean or pea shoots

THE VEGAN BARBIE

The barbecue season – as with other seasonal food traditions – can seem like a bit of a challenge when you're on a plant-based diet, but there are plenty of ways you can enjoy an al fresco get-together with your family and friends, without going hungry.

Take your own BBQ – this saves a lot of hassle and worries about cross-contamination. Just pick up a disposable barbecue on the way and take along your own tongs, etc. (You may want to let your host know, first.)

Take your own stash of mains – you'll be supplying a lot of this BBQ fare yourself, but it's better to have plenty of options than to go hungry. Some easy things to pop on the grill include: asparagus (pre-soaked), corn on the cob, pineapples slices, portobello mushrooms, tempeh or tofu (marinated), veggie kebabs, veggie sausages and/or burgers, and apples, bananas and dark chocolate (wrapped in foil).

Take some tasty sides to share – as you'll be cooking separately, sharing some side dishes is a nice way to bond with your fellow guests. A chunky home-made new potato salad, dressed with chives or spring onions and some vegan mayo, is simple to prepare and filling too.

Get creative – you can make your own 'hot dog' by grilling some marinated tofu and serving it in a roll with mustard and ketchup – and when it comes to vegan burger options, you'll be spoilt for choice. Whether you choose an off-the-shelf pack of patties or make your own veggie-based ones, don't forget to dress your burger with vegan cheese slices, pickles, salad, relish or guacamole.

SOCIALISING

Dinner-party Tips

- If you're going for coffee, take a bottle of plant-based milk with you and leave it in the fridge – your friends might be converted!

- Taking along some 'accidentally' vegan snacks is also a good move. (Familiar items, such as Oreos, go down well.)

- Phone ahead if it's a dinner party and let your host know that you're vegan. They may be happy to provide some plant-based side dishes while you bring along a vegan main to share, for example.

- If your hosts have made the effort to make something vegan, be positive and supportive.

- Have some dark chocolate in your bag for a sweet fix after your meal, just in case there are no vegan options on the menu – or take along your favourite vegan dessert to share.

- If you have children who are vegan and they're invited to a party, taking a couple of platters of vegan bakes or party food is a nice gesture and will ensure that your little one has something to eat. (You might want to reassure them that there will be some vegan cake or sweets waiting for them at home, as chances are the party boy or girl will be handing out non-vegan party bags!)

The Only Vegan in the Room?

When you change your diet, you suddenly realise that most social events revolve around eating or drinking together, and it won't be long before someone asks you a little more about your vegan lifestyle. Often people will be positive, but if a fellow guest asks one question too many, just direct them to your favourite vegan website, saying that they can find out more online if they're interested.

EATING OUT AND ABOUT

More and more restaurants are vegan friendly these days, but plan ahead and you'll enjoy eating out without having to compromise on taste or your principles!

- If you know where you're going ahead of time, it makes sense to check out the menu online or phone in advance to see what options are available.

- If you know that you're going for a particular type of cuisine, check online for some general ideas about which dishes might be best for you. (The Veganuary website has some good suggestions.)

- If you feel self-conscious about quizzing the waiting staff in front of your companions, excuse yourself and have a chat with them away from your table.

- If there are no obvious vegan meals, start by asking for the vegetarian menu and see if you can work out any options from there.

- Mix and match side dishes or starters, if there's no vegan main dish available; some veggie sides are really delicious.

- If you think you'll be going hungry, eat something before you meet up, so that you can enjoy a snack and a drink alongside your dinner companions.

Travel Tips

* Search for vegan-friendly accommodation, or stay somewhere with your own kitchen (check Airbnb, for instance) or fridge so you can keep a few supplies in your room. Let your hosts know in advance that you're vegan and they may provide some plant-based milk for you.

* Keep vegan snacks in your bag, and pack a few little lidded tubs so that you can take leftovers away with you to munch on later.

* Pack herbal teabags (in case there's no plant milk available) and keep a small bottle of your favourite dressing or sauce in your bag (in case salad is the only vegan option on the menu).

* Social media is your friend: search for #vegantravel on Instagram. Pinterest is also a great resource. Check out vegan travel blogs and vegan communities local to your destination.

* Learn a few phrases in the language of your destination country – questions such as: 'Is there meat/milk/egg in that?' are obviously useful when asking for food. You can print out the most helpful and carry them in your wallet or purse. (The Vegan Society's 'Vegan Passport' includes useful phrases in over 70 languages and is also available as an app.)

A CLEAN KITCHEN

Your kitchen is filled with vegan-friendly foods, but how do you go about keeping it clean without using products that contain animal derivatives or have been tested on animals? A surprising number of detergents and other products contain animal fats, but these are often listed by their chemical names and therefore difficult to spot – and when it comes to animal testing, it can be a bit of a minefield. Don't worry, though. There are two sure-fire ways to make sure that your kitchen products are vegan-friendly: look for cruelty-free brands or make your own.

There are some great guaranteed vegan-friendly brands. Dr Bronner's multipurpose cleaner is super effective (and super concentrated), and can be used for everything from laundry to surface/floor cleaning and doing the dishes. The Method range is also a safe choice, and so is Astonish (whose products won't break the bank). Many supermarkets' own brands are vegan-friendly too; check online for more details.

Label Lookout

Products marked with the Leaping Bunny or the PETA bunny logos (see p.157) have not been tested on animals, and if something is labelled 'free from animal ingredients' or 'entirely plant-based', you can be sure that its components are vegan-friendly. If the wording used is 'never tested on animals', though, there is no guarantee that some of its individual elements haven't been tested on animals. Products marked with accredited vegan logos tick both boxes – no animal testing or unwanted ingredients.

The second option is to make your own cleaning products using natural ingredients, and the bonus is that you'll avoid using chemicals and additives in your kitchen. So why not try making:

Oven cleaner with 90 g baking soda and 2–3 tbsp water. Mix to make a paste, apply to your oven – but not the heating element – and leave overnight. Wipe away the next morning with a damp cloth and finish by spraying the oven with some white vinegar, before giving it a final wipe.

Fridge freshener by popping half a lemon in a bowl of bicarbonate of soda and leaving in the fridge to remove any odours.

Floor cleaner with equal parts white vinegar and water.

Surface cleanser by putting a solution of 125 ml white vinegar and 2 tbsp baking soda into a spray bottle. Pop in a few drops of your favourite essential oil (tea tree works well) and top the bottle up with water.

Toilet cleaner by combining 250 ml white vinegar with $\frac{1}{2}$ tsp of tea tree oil in a spray bottle. Squirt inside the toilet bowl and leave for a few minutes. Then sprinkle 90 g baking soda over the area and scrub. Use the vinegar/tea tree oil mix alone to wipe down the lid and handle.

Window cleaner by using equal parts water and white vinegar, mixed in a spray bottle. Wipe off with newspaper for a streak-free finish.

AN ECO-FRIENDLY KITCHEN

Laundry Detergent

As with your other kitchen products, you'll want to find a detergent that's cruelty-free, but you might also want to consider the impact that its ingredients could have when they find their way into the water cycle. Picking something that's 100 per cent biodegradable and non-toxic is important, so either opt for an eco-friendly brand (such as Ecover, Method, Astonish or Earth Friendly) or get creative and make your own DIY laundry products.

- Grate a bar of Castile soap, and mix in ½ a cup of soda crystals and ½ a cup of borax to make your own laundry detergent. Use 1 tbsp per load (or 2 tbsp if clothes are more heavily soiled).

- Make your own fabric softener by filling a jar with white vinegar and adding a splash of your favourite essential oil. Use the same amount as you would for a shop-bought brand to soften your clothes and leave them smelling sweet – and don't worry, your garments won't smell of vinegar!

- Give soap nuts a try – these naturally grown, biodegradable nuts will produce soap suds in contact with water. Just pop half a dozen in a net bag and put them in the washing machine with your laundry load.

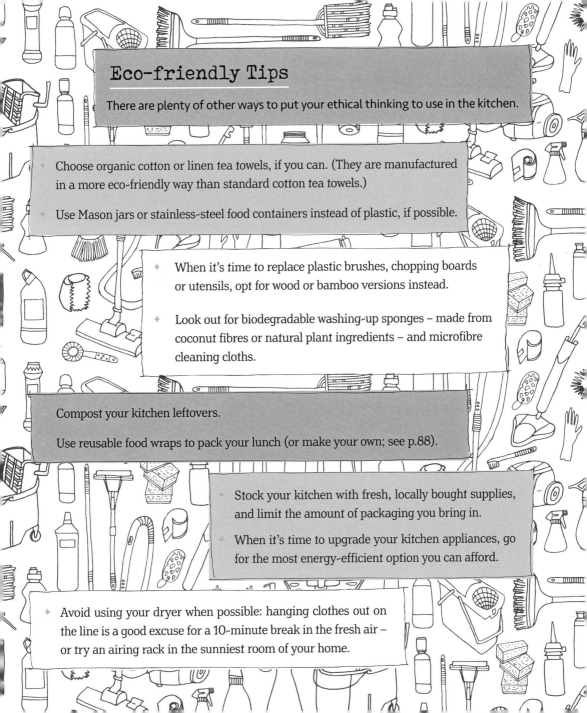

Eco-friendly Tips

There are plenty of other ways to put your ethical thinking to use in the kitchen.

- Choose organic cotton or linen tea towels, if you can. (They are manufactured in a more eco-friendly way than standard cotton tea towels.)

- Use Mason jars or stainless-steel food containers instead of plastic, if possible.

- When it's time to replace plastic brushes, chopping boards or utensils, opt for wood or bamboo versions instead.

- Look out for biodegradable washing-up sponges – made from coconut fibres or natural plant ingredients – and microfibre cleaning cloths.

Compost your kitchen leftovers.

Use reusable food wraps to pack your lunch (or make your own; see p.88).

- Stock your kitchen with fresh, locally bought supplies, and limit the amount of packaging you bring in.

- When it's time to upgrade your kitchen appliances, go for the most energy-efficient option you can afford.

- Avoid using your dryer when possible: hanging clothes out on the line is a good excuse for a 10-minute break in the fresh air – or try an airing rack in the sunniest room of your home.

MAKE YOUR OWN REUSABLE FOOD WRAPS

If you want to avoid using cling film or foil, reusable food wraps are a must, but many shop-bought ones are coated in beeswax. Here's how you can make your own vegan food wraps at home.

You will need:

100 per cent cotton fabric
Pinking shears
A few tablespoons of soya wax pieces
Greaseproof paper
An iron and ironing board

1. Use pinking shears to cut your fabric into rough squares of whatever size will be useful to you.

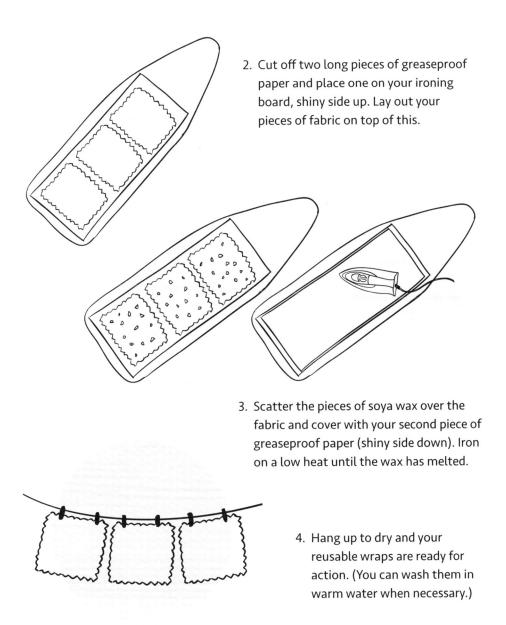

2. Cut off two long pieces of greaseproof paper and place one on your ironing board, shiny side up. Lay out your pieces of fabric on top of this.

3. Scatter the pieces of soya wax over the fabric and cover with your second piece of greaseproof paper (shiny side down). Iron on a low heat until the wax has melted.

4. Hang up to dry and your reusable wraps are ready for action. (You can wash them in warm water when necessary.)

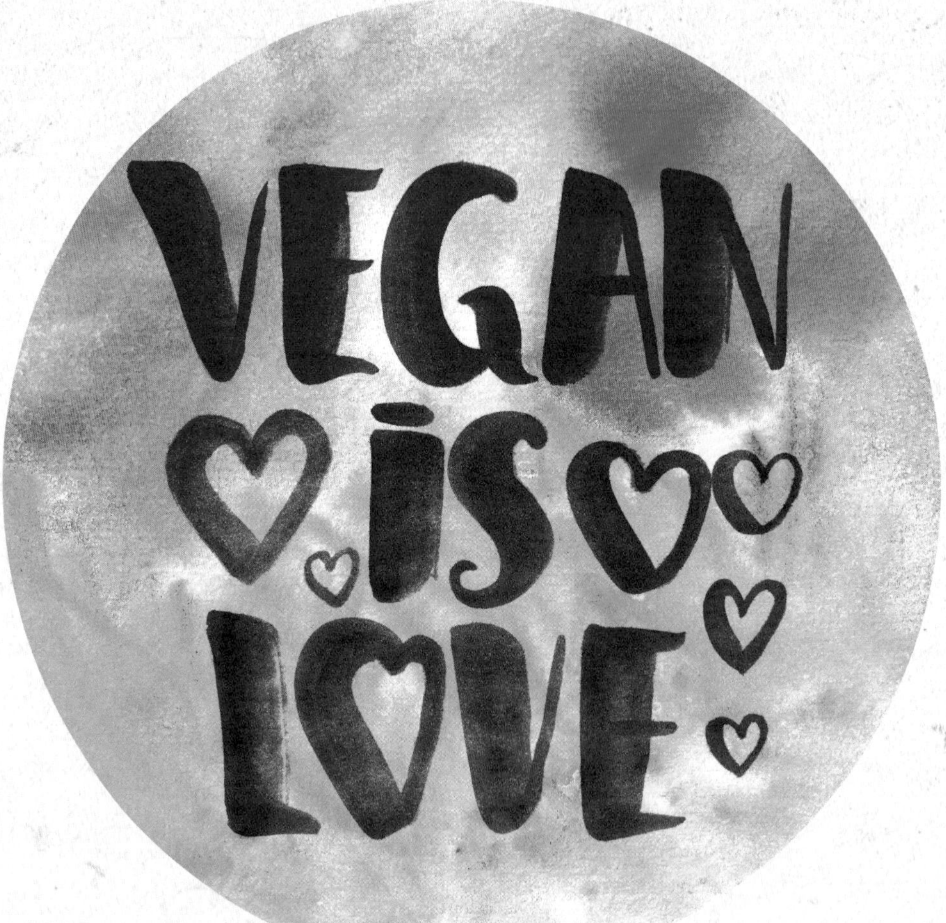
VEGAN
IS
LOVE

CHAPTER THREE

VEGAN LIVING AND HOME

There are plenty of ways to extend your compassionate choices to the rest of your home, from fabrics and furniture to gardening and pet care. It's almost impossible to have a completely vegan home – and often impractical to remove all your non-vegan items in one go – but you may want to pick an area to update. You could think about veganising your bedding or replacing that old leather sofa, for example. Every ethical decision or effort you make is a step in the right direction and will make a difference.

MATERIAL CONCERNS

Vegans prefer to avoid using materials that have come from animals. This can make home furnishing seem like a challenge at first but, as with stocking your fridge, once you've sussed out what to avoid – and found some reliable suppliers of alternatives – you'll be able to make ethical choices in every room.

The main culprits to avoid in home furnishings are leather (and suede), wool (and felt), silk, down, fur and cowhide. The production of each of these materials is – unfortunately – inherently cruel (most animal welfare websites will give you more information on why). The good news is that there are plenty of ways to make compassionate choices when you're picking soft furnishings, and they needn't break the bank.

Throws

Avoid wool and opt for acrylic or other synthetic fibres (which are just as cosy), or use blankets made from recycled materials.

Silk Production

In order to produce silk, silkworms are farmed and then boiled during their pupal stage, so that the thread can be retrieved from the cocoons. To produce just 1 g of silk thread, 15 silkworms are killed, so imagine the huge numbers that need to be destroyed for the production of large pieces of silk cloth.

Curtains and Rugs

Jute is a great option for rugs, but there are plenty of other good non-wool alternatives out there such as synthetic fibres. You can even find curtains made from hemp. (See p.118 for more on the choice of textiles; if you're unsure about a material listed, check out www.compassionatecloset.com for a database of fabrics and their vegan/non-vegan status.)

Cushions

Think about the cushion filling, as well as the cover material. Don't opt for down: polyester is a cruelty-free alternative. (Some companies specialise in making cushions from recycled materials, so check these out online.)

Sofas

If the leather or cowhide look appeals to you, you can easily track down faux versions online. When choosing a new couch, remember that you'll need to consider the padding materials as well as the cover. Amazon is a good place to find vegan sofas, as well as Ikea – while some options are a little more expensive than others, the latter offer affordable memory-foam-based vegan sofas, so you don't need to take out a mortgage in order to sit in comfort!

 # FURNITURE

If you're buying a new item of furniture for your home – particularly something made from wood – you've got a great opportunity to make a difference to the environment with some ethical shopping. Here are some things to bear in mind when searching for your new coffee table... or dining chairs... or wardrobe... or...

Buy Sustainably Sourced Wood

Deforestation is a huge environmental issue that has a direct impact on the lives of thousands of creatures and is a major contributor to global warming, so if you're buying a new item, picking wood that has been sustainably harvested is a must. If furniture is certified with the FSC mark – the 'tick tree' logo – you'll know you're on safe ground.

Think Reclaimed or Recycled

Furniture made from reclaimed wood is another great option: look out for the Rainforest Alliance's 'Rediscovered Wood' certification on these items, but any reclaimed or recycled option is better than buying something new. If you're creative, perhaps you can upcycle something yourself with a lick of (cruelty-free) paint.

It is estimated that an area of rainforest the size
of 20 football pitches is cut down every minute
(for clearance, agriculture and timber usage).

Buy Bamboo

Bamboo is a really versatile material that can be made into furniture, flooring or blinds (and smaller items of kitchenware). It is a grass – not a tree – and is incredibly fast-growing, so it's a resource that's easily replenished.

Go for Something Vintage

Things that were made back in the day were made to last, so here's your opportunity to give an older item a new lease of life and embrace the vintage trend in your home. You can find some lovely pieces of furniture at second-hand shops or charity outlets. You'll be drawing on zero resources in terms of manufacturing and may well be saving your chosen piece from landfill, too.

Think Ahead

Try to buy items that are versatile, as well as practical and future-proof – perhaps your computer desk could become a small kitchen table, if you upsize? As a rule, try to avoid items that are a mixture of too many different types of materials, as these won't be easy to recycle in the future. Pieces that can be disassembled for the separate parts to be recycled are more eco-friendly.

KEEPING IT CLEAN

Many cleaning products don't have great cruelty-free credentials, but it's perfectly possible to make your own natural versions so that you can be sure of their ingredients (see p.85). When it comes to caring for your wooden furniture, it's easy to make polish, so you can avoid any beeswax-based products. You can also choose wisely when it comes to cleaning cloths and brushes.

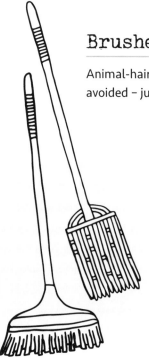

Brushes and Brooms

Animal-hair brushes and brooms are easily avoided – just pick synthetic ones instead.

Cleaning Cloths

Opt for microfibre or wood-fibre cloths, as these are biodegradable (and easily findable too!). Above all, remember to avoid using single-use wipes to clean furniture, as they are so detrimental to the environment.

Dusters

Feather and lambswool dusters are a no-no, but alternatives are widely available and just as effective – microfibre dusters even create their own electrostatic charge that attracts dust, rather than sending it whirling off into the air.

Make Your Own Polish

It's easy to bring a natural shine to your furniture and floors without the use of beeswax or harsh chemicals.

For Furniture

You could use 180 ml olive oil mixed with 60 ml fresh lemon juice (or vinegar): apply and polish with a soft rag. Or how about choosing coconut oil? You can simply lightly dab a small amount on your cloth to gather the dust and give furniture a gentle polish. Alternatively, melt 30 g in a pan and add a couple of teaspoons of lemon juice for a sweet-smelling, all-natural sheen.

For Wooden Floors

The cleaning power of vinegar works well on wooden floors, too, so mix up a solution of (roughly) one part vinegar to ten parts warm water in your bucket, and mop to clean and shine in one fell swoop.

BEDROOM

It's surprising that even mattresses can contain animal products, but rest assured that it is possible to veganise your bedroom and enjoy a cruelty-free night's sleep. As is the case for virtually any aspect of a vegan lifestyle, with a little detective work you can learn what to look for and hunt down some animal-friendly options.

Mattresses

Latex mattresses can contain casein (which is derived from milk); others can be wadded with wool, and even the glue holding them together can be animal-derived. This is an area where an internet search is the only way to guarantee that what you're buying is vegan-friendly. The good news is that there are dozens of suppliers who realise the importance of offering vegan options – cotton mattresses or those filled with buckwheat are good options. The latter should last for ten years or so, and when the time comes to replace them, they are biodegradable, so you won't be adding to landfill.

Duvets and Pillows

Down (soft feathers taken from ducks and geese) is an obvious no-no, but vegan-friendly options to look out for include: cotton, hollowfibre, microfibre, buckwheat or kapok. Memory-foam pillows are another alternative.

Bedding

Bamboo-blend sheets look very similar to silk, and are a good eco-friendly choice too. If cotton sheets are on your list, go for organic, where possible, to avoid the eco-issues that come with buying the standard type. Textiles marked with the GOTS label are certified organic, and Fairtrade items have been sourced and manufactured in an ethical way.

Watch out for products that are labelled 'all natural', as these may not be vegan-friendly. They could contain wool or silk.

❦ DECORATIVE TOUCHES

Paints

There are a few issues to consider when you're choosing paint for your home, such as whether or not the manufacturer tests products on animals – and this is usually fairly easy to investigate – and if the products themselves contain milk derivatives (casein) or beeswax as a binder. With a product labelled 'vegan' you're on safe ground, but 'natural' and 'eco-friendly' provide no guarantees. Finding vegan paint can be a bit of a challenge, but one or two manufacturers are leading the way and labelling their products clearly, so sticking to those for the time being (or doing a little online research into other brands) is your best option.

Compassionate Art

It's not just the paints that you use to decorate your home that include non-vegan ingredients. Artists' paints commonly contain everything from ox gall to crushed insects or bones, and canvases are often treated with gelatine or fixed with animal-derived glues. Fortunately, some art supplies manufacturers do not use animal products in their ranges – such as Blick and Faber-Castell (except for their crayons) – while others are largely safe (e.g. Holbein). You can also source paintbrushes that are not made from animal hair. A quick internet search for cruelty-free art supplies will reveal plenty of options so you can get creative with a clean conscience.

And Don't Forget

The items that we use to decorate our homes can often include animal-derived components, so it's good to bear this in mind when you next buy something from the homeware department.

Candles are one example. Many use beeswax as a component, and the ingredients aren't always listed on the label, so it can be difficult to check. Soy-based candles are a great alternative – and you can even make your own very easily (see p.102).

How far you want to go when veganising your home is up to you. It's pretty easy to keep a checklist of materials to avoid in mind, and you might find them cropping up in unexpected places when it comes to home décor (some ornaments use leather or silk cords, for example).

You might want to think about the materials used to craft items, too. The glue used to découpage pictures could well be animal-derived, for example, and gilded pieces are very likely to have had the gilt applied with an ox-hair brush. These sorts of decisions are personal ones and only you can determine your own feelings about including certain objects in your home.

Many vegans are quite happy to bring back found seashells for crafting or to decorate their house, but would prefer not to buy items that have seashells as a component, for example, as they can't guarantee how these have been sourced.

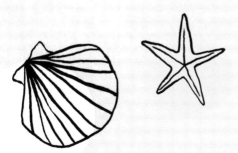

Other things to avoid:

- Coral
- Feathers
- Furs
- Horn
- Ivory
- Seashells
- Taxidermy (of course!)

MAKE YOUR OWN SOY CANDLES

These cruelty-free candles are a lovely way to enhance your home, and they make great gifts, too. You can use any heatproof glass or ceramic container for your creations and even custom-mix your favourite essential oils to add fragrance to them.

Mason jars,
heatproof glasses
or ceramic bowls

Soy wax flakes

Glass bowl

Tabbed wicks

Glue dots

Essential oil

TIP:

Remove any bubbles on the surface of your candle by gently heating with a hairdryer and allowing to cool down again.

For each candle:

1. Measure out your wax flakes: fill your container to an inch below the top and pour the flakes into a glass bowl. You'll need to double this quantity for one candle, so repeat the process and you'll have exactly the right amount of wax.

2. Pop a glue dot on the bottom of a wick and press this down into the centre of your container. (Use a pencil or chopstick if it's tricky to reach).

3. Melt your wax, stirring occasionally. You can do this in the microwave, but if you set your bowl on top of a saucepan, you can keep an eye on it as it melts.

4. Once the wax is liquid, carefully remove from the heat and allow to cool for a few minutes. Then add your essential oil and stir thoroughly. The amount you need will vary, as some scents are stronger than others, but approximately 30 drops for a small candle or 50 for a larger Mason jar are good guides.

5. Carefully pour the wax into the container – use a clothes peg (or your handy pencil or popsicle stick) to keep the wick standing straight while you do that.

6. Leave the candle to cool overnight, trim the wick down to half an inch above the level of the wax and you're ready to go.

COMPANION ANIMALS

Many of us love to share our lives (and households) with animal companions, so – when you're veganising your lifestyle – you might wonder how you can improve the way you look after your pet. From the care products you buy to the food that you feed them, there are always little tweaks you can make to ensure that your pet is living in the most eco-friendly way possible.

Thinking it Through

If you haven't yet chosen your companion, here are a few common-sense pointers to consider before you begin.

- Make sure you're going to be able to give your pet enough space and attention to keep them happy.

- Visit a rescue centre and rehome an animal that is in need rather than visiting a breeder.

- Make sure that you have your pet neutered, so that you don't end up overrun with unexpected furry companions!

- Think about diet – if feeding your animal meat-based products is an issue, then cats, dogs, snakes, ferrets and some types of aquarium fish may not be for you.

Rabbits
Rodents
Small fish
Guinea pigs
Birds

It can be uncomfortable seeing birds in cages, but many animal lovers rescue pets that have been abandoned or badly treated. (This is true, too, for ex-battery chickens.)

Eco-friendly Kit

When you're buying supplies for your pet, you can make a huge difference to the environment by thinking about the materials you're investing in. Many pet products are made of plastic – particularly toys, bowls and toileting paraphernalia – and these items are often packaged in additional plastic. There are several companies that offer more eco-friendly options so it's almost always possible to make a wiser decision: you can choose bamboo food bowls and litter trays, as well as opting for wood-based cat litter and buying biodegradable poop bags, for example.

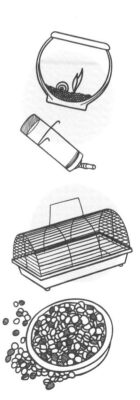

ψ PET FOOD

Cats, dogs, ferrets and snakes do need a certain amount of meat in their diet to meet their nutritional needs, although in some cases it is possible to feed your animal home-made food and supplement this. There's no reason why your pet can't enjoy more vegetables in their diet and benefit from your new regime: try adding a spoonful or two of veggies to their usual food, but make sure you don't include any no-go ingredients (see below). It's always best to check with your vet before you change your pet's diet.

DOG		CAT	
Asparagus	Apples*	Cheese	Banana
Avocado	Bananas	Grapes and raisins	Blueberries
Cherries	Blueberries and strawberries	Milk	Broccoli (cooked)
Citrus fruits	Brussels sprouts	Onions and garlic	Carrots (cooked)
Garlic and onions	Carrots		Cucumber
Grapes and raisins	Green beans		Green beans
Macadamia nuts	Pumpkin		Pumpkin
Peaches, persimmons, plums	Spinach		Squash
Anything too salty or sweet	Sweet potato		Watermelon*
	Watermelon*		

*Remove the seeds first, as these may make your animal unwell.

Vegan Pupsicles

Making these frozen treats for your dog to enjoy on a hot day is a great alternative to giving them processed snack food – and you'll be cutting down on packaging, too.

You will need:

- Dog-friendly fruit, such as blueberries, chopped apples, bananas or strawberries
- Vegetable broth or stock (make sure it does not contain onions or garlic)
- Edible handle – peeled carrot or celery sticks

Method

1. Line up some small containers suitable to go in the freezer and scatter in some chopped-up fruit.

2. Pour in some broth, leaving an inch or so at the top (so that your lolly doesn't overflow when you put the stick in).

3. Pop in the carrot or celery sticks and freeze for 2–3 hours.

4. Remove from the container and watch your dog enjoy their treat!

VEGANIC GARDENING

The decisions you make when gardening will have a direct impact on the ecosystem right outside your door, so you can really benefit your local wildlife with some ethical choices. Veganic gardening – a combined vegan and organic approach – means not using any sprays, pesticides or chemicals on your patch, as well as avoiding all animal-based manures and fertilisers. As with veganising other areas of your home, take your journey one step at a time, and you'll soon enjoy the benefits of organic produce and a garden bursting with biodiversity. Here are a few areas where you can make some changes.

COMPOST BIN
IN USE

Enhancing Your Soil

Most commercially bought soil additives include animal products of some kind – blood and bone meal, fish meal and other animal-derived components – so try out some natural soil enhancers instead.

Make your own compost using your fruit and veg peelings, grass clippings, and green garden waste.

Grow green manures by planting fast-growing crops – such as rye, buckwheat or corn – and then digging them into the soil to retain and return nutrients.

Fix nitrogen by periodically planting lupins, peas or broad beans in your veggie patch.

Make your own fertiliser by mixing one part kelp meal, two parts cottonseed meal, two parts rock phosphate and three parts wood ash or greensand.

Find shop-bought alternatives to traditional composts and manures: think kelp, cottonseed or soya bean, or check with your local garden centre to see what they have available.

Treat your plants to a dose of nettle tea: put some bruised nettle leaves and stems into a bucket and top up with rainwater, leaving a little room at the top for the fertiliser to brew. Cover and leave somewhere sunny for two weeks to ferment, stirring every couple of days. Finally, strain out the nettles and dilute your brew to one part nettle tea to six parts water. Use to water tubs, baskets, veg and salad crops.

Some vegans are happy to use manure that has come from horses or cattle on a local smallholding rather than purchasing commercial manures, so this may be an option for you.

ᛘ VEGAN PRODUCE

One of the best benefits of veganic gardening is that you can have a supply of your own organic crops to enjoy. It makes sense to produce the things that you love to eat, so do a little research and find out whether your favourite vegan staples can be grown where you live. As always, the internet is chock-full of advice, and gardeners are friendly and knowledgeable folk who are happy to share their tips. So whether it's your own supply of window-box salads or herbs, or a crop of soya beans or quinoa that tempts you to get your spade out, you'll be able to find lots of information on how to get a bumper harvest.

Top 5 Vegan Crops to Grow for Beginners

1. Salad leaves
2. Berries
3. Root veggies
4. Herbs
5. Tomatoes

Keeping Pests at Bay

By avoiding the use of pesticides, you're upholding your ethical principles and making sure that your produce is organic at the same time. Here are a few ways you can keep your crops safe without getting the chemical sprays out.

1. Identify your pest: first of all, find out what's nibbling your cabbages so that you can deter it accordingly!

2. Gardening in raised beds or low fencing can keep your crops out of the way of ground-based mammals.

3. Use netting or old-fashioned scarecrow-type deterrents to scare off birds.

4. Distract pests with a few sacrificial plants, an open compost container or the odd half-a-grapefruit dotted around the garden to feed the slugs.

5. Cut plastic bottles or cartons into rings to pop over your seedlings until they are established.

6. Practise scatter planting: rather than dedicating a large expanse to one crop, dot veggies around, mixing in a range of herbs and flowers to confuse pests and stop them from zeroing in on one particular crop in one go.

7. Try companion planting: plant garlic or onions alongside carrots to deter carrot fly, for example, or tomatoes alongside cabbages to repel the moths that snack on their leaves.

8. Encourage frogs and toads into your garden with a small pond. These creatures love to snack on slugs and might take care of your pest control for you.

MAKE A WILDLIFE STACK

Encourage animals into your garden by building a wildlife hotel using found materials, as well as repurposed pots and pallets. You'll be offering shelter to all sorts of critters that will add to the biodiversity of your backyard.

You will need:

Old wooden pallets or crates

Planks and strips of wood

Old terracotta pots or roofing tiles

A sheet of roofing felt

Natural materials: pine cones, moss, hollow plant stems, bark, twigs, straw and dry leaves

1. First of all, prepare your site: a square of level ground (away from your veggie patch) is best.

2. Next, build your basic structure. If you're using pallets, space them out with bricks in between and add a layer of tiles or wood for a solid 'floor' now and then. Use a few bricks around the outer edges to keep your structure sturdy, too. (You can make a smaller stack with wooden crates or boxes.)

3. Fill in the layers with natural materials as you go. Different things will attract different residents: wood and bark will encourage beetles and woodlice to settle in; bunches of hollow stems (or trimmed garden canes) are great for ladybirds or lone bees; and holes between tiles and stones will be the perfect home for frogs and toads.

4. Finish your hotel with a piece of roofing felt held down by bricks to keep the inhabitants dry, and – if you're feeling really industrious – plant some buddleia, lavender and other nectar-rich plants nearby so that your visitors will have a handy supply of food.

Short on Space?

If you don't have room for a large structure, why not fill a
terracotta pot with trimmed garden canes or a bunch of cut
hollow plant stems? Position somewhere warm and dry (on its
side with the top angled downwards, so that the canes won't
fill with water) and you've got the perfect hideaway for bees or
ladybirds. Even a bundle of sticks or twigs tied with string and left
in the shade will make a good home for beetles and woodlice.

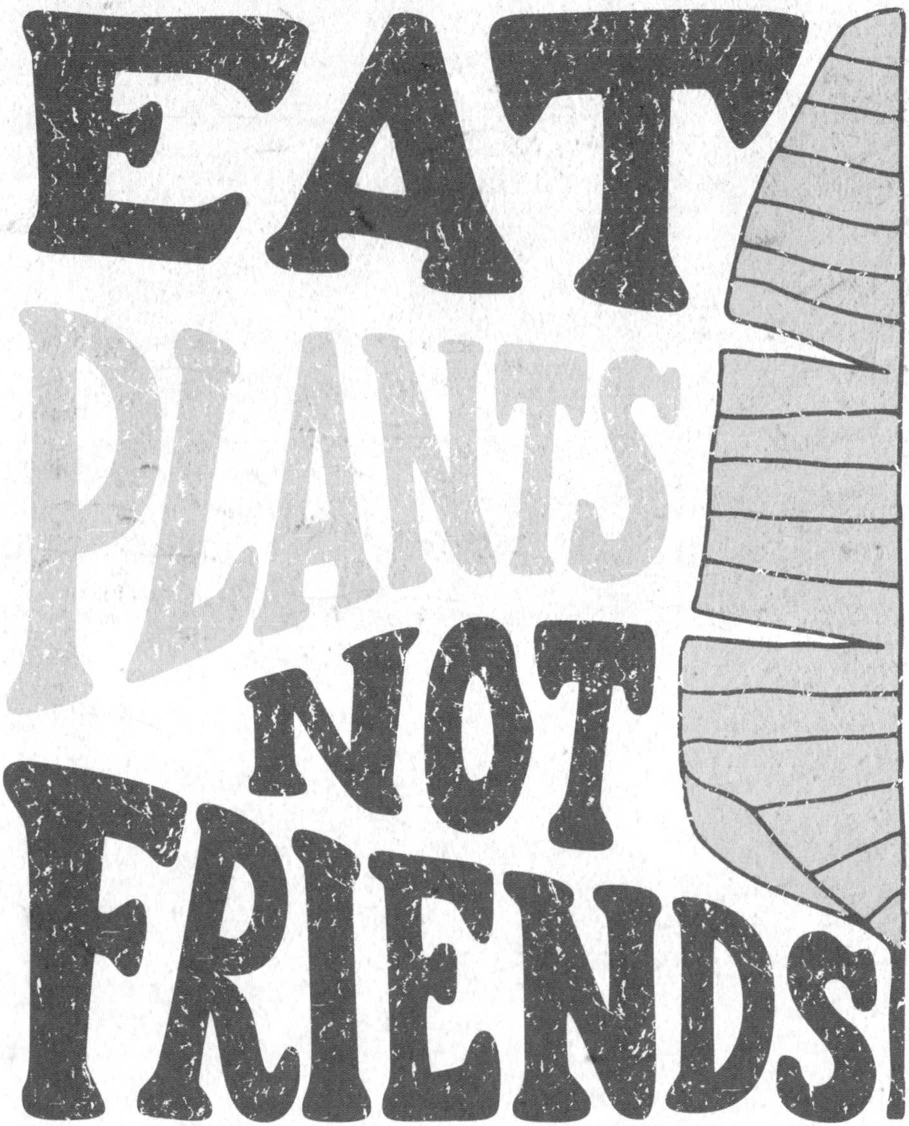
EAT
PLANTS
NOT
FRIENDS

CHAPTER FOUR

THE VEGAN WARDROBE

Many people like to rethink their wardrobe when they become vegan. The clothes we wear say a lot about us – and, of course, we spend a lot of time in them too! – so it's natural to want to move away from animal-derived materials and embrace vegan clothing. From clever alternatives to leather and vegan-friendly stores on the high street, to repurposed jewellery and cruelty-free accessories, there are now more easy ways to veganise your look than ever before.

CRUELTY-FREE CLOTHING

Choosing vegan clothes is easy once you know what to look out for, and a simple first step is to decide not to purchase any new items made from animal-derived materials. There are so many alternatives available that often look identical, but are a cruelty-free option. In some cases, vegan fabrics can come at a bit of a price, but remember that by simply avoiding the materials listed in the first column of the table overleaf, and choosing organic cotton or man-made fabrics instead, you're upholding your vegan principles.

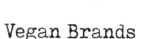

Vegan Brands

The huge demand for ethical clothing is reflected in the number of top designers who are using vegan alternatives to leather and dropping fur from their collections, including Stella McCartney, Donatella Versace and Gucci. Many high-street stores are moving away from wool and refuse to sell fur or angora. Check out the PETA website for their list of vegan-friendly retailers, which includes H&M, Zara and bebe, among many others.

Label Lookout

These logos all denote vegan items:

- PETA-Approved Vegan – for clothing and accessories
- Vegan Trademark (the Vegan Society's sunflower symbol)
- V-label (in the EU)
- Certified Vegan Logo (in the US).

If an item is marked 'man-made material', it is a good sign that it's cruelty-free, but watch out for fabric blends (e.g. 80 per cent acrylic and 20 per cent mohair).

Making the Transition

As with adapting your diet, how you make the transition to a vegan wardrobe is down to you. You may decide to continue to use what you already have, and replace garments when you need them with cruelty-free items. Or perhaps you would like to get rid of some larger items – leather jackets and silk scarves – straight away. Some people like to go all-out and veganise their wardrobe in one go.

Another decision to make is what to do with the items that you're replacing. Everyone's opinion is different, so see how you feel: many people prefer to donate them to charity, rather than seeing them end up in landfill, as doing so does not increase demand for these goods. You could give clothing to a homeless shelter or wildlife charity shop, or pass on woollens to an animal sanctuary to be used as bedding.

MATERIAL MATTERS

Avoid this...	... and go for this instead
Conventional cotton: although it's plant-based, its production can be very detrimental to the environment	Organic cotton or linen; hemp; SeaCell (a material made from ground seaweed fibre)
Felt made from wool	Polymer felt (which is often made from recycled plastic bottles)
Fur	Faux fur
Leather and suede	Polyurethane; vegan leather (including pineapple, mushroom and apple-fibre leather); microfibre suede
Silk	Artificial silk; modal (a soft, silky fabric made from renewable fibre from beech trees); soybean fabric
Traditional velvet (often made from silk)	Most velvets nowadays are made from synthetic fabrics, which are much more durable than silk-based versions
Wool and wool mixes (including alpaca, angora, cashmere, lambskin, llama, mohair, pashm and shearling)	Lyocell (a biodegradable material made from wood pulp); hemp; organic cotton; linen; SeaCell

Other fabrics that are cruelty-free: bamboo, Cupro, denim, Lycra, nylon, polyester, rayon, satin, Tencel and viscose.

You can identify faux fur by looking for stitching on the fabric backing and for a consistent, regular pattern. It also feels more like carpet material, whereas real fur feels like hair and tapers to a point.

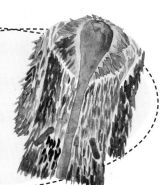

Cruelty-free Cotton

Cotton is vegan-friendly, but when you're investing in new clothes, look for the organic option. Conventional cotton is cultivated using chemicals that damage the environment and its production often involves exploitative labour. Cotton production is highly water intensive, too, and this can wreak havoc on local communities and ecosystems.

It can take 20,000 litres of water to produce 1 kg of cotton: the amount used to make one T-shirt and a pair of jeans.

ACCESSORIES AND ACCOUTREMENTS

Don't forget the details when you're making sure that your wardrobe is cruelty free. Think about the materials used for buttons and trims on garments and bags, for example. Jewellery often includes animal-derived products, too. Veganising your wardrobe is a great opportunity to declutter and to consider your look at the same time: you're choosing to champion ethical living, and the way you present yourself is one of the most direct means of doing so. What you wear really counts.

Materials such as **alligator skin** and **snakeskin** can turn up on shoes or bags, alongside leather, of course. Go for synthetic, man-made options instead.

Pearls (and mother-of-pearl) are used in jewellery and accessories, and as buttons. It's almost impossible to tell if they are fake or not, unless you're an expert, but vintage items are more likely to be problematic.

Tortoiseshell could crop up on items picked up at charity shops. The real deal has irregular markings, whereas synthetic items tend to have regular patterns.

Down (or feathers) can be used to fill winter coats, so check the labels before buying.

Animal bones and teeth are used in jewellery, and some buttons on vintage garments are made from animal horn.

Feathers are used on hats and in jewellery, not to mention feather boas... but there aren't many occasions where one of those is required!

Leather is not just used for shoes and bags, but also for labels on jeans, straps and cords in watches, and pulls on zips.

Jewellery can include pearl, mother-of-pearl, coral, horn and ivory – but, of course, it doesn't need to. Beads, crystals, faux pearls and metal items are all safe alternatives. If you're thinking of investing in jewellery that includes precious stones, such as diamonds, do some research first to make sure they're traceable to an ethical source, and buy Fairtrade gold if you can.

UPCYCLED BRACELET

Making your own jewellery from repurposed beaded necklaces and bracelets is very satisfying and eco-friendly – and, of course, you can ensure that the materials you use are cruelty-free, too. You can pick up second-hand items very cheaply at charity shops and have fun finding different colours that will work well together. Upcycled jewellery also makes the perfect ethical gift. You can buy jewellery tools, wire and findings very cheaply at craft stores or online.

You will need:

Second-hand beaded necklaces or bracelets

Wire cutters

Flexible beading wire

A magnetic or toggle clasp

2 crimp beads, to fit your wire

Findings, e.g. spacer beads, jump rings and metal charms, if wanted

Pointed pliers

1. Start by removing the beads from their original settings. Use the wire cutters to clip the end of the necklace or bracelet you've chosen, and sort the beads into small dishes to make threading easier.

2. Measure a piece of beading wire to a length of about 25 cm and clip off with the cutters. (Use a wire that will fit through the hole in your repurposed beads twice.)

3. Slide one of the crimp beads on to one end of the wire, followed by one half of the clasp. Poke the end of the wire back through the crimp bead to make a loop around the clasp, which should be held in place with a little gap, so that it can move around. Use the pliers to crimp (squash) the bead securely.

4. Next, thread on the decorative beads in your chosen pattern, from the free end of your wire, adding spacer beads if you like. (Thread the first few over the looped-over excess wire and then clip this end off.) When the bracelet is the right length for your wrist, pop on the other crimp bead and the other half of the clasp. Secure the latter by threading the wire back through the crimp bead and tightening, sliding the crimp bead down to sit at the end of the beads.

5. Squash the crimp bead firmly into place. Thread the excess wire back down through a few beads by using your pliers and then trim off with the wire cutters.

6. Use the pliers to attach a charm to your bracelet with a jump ring, if you like. (It's usually easiest to fit one in next to the clasp.)

TIP:

The label on the wire will indicate
the size of crimp bead that you should use.

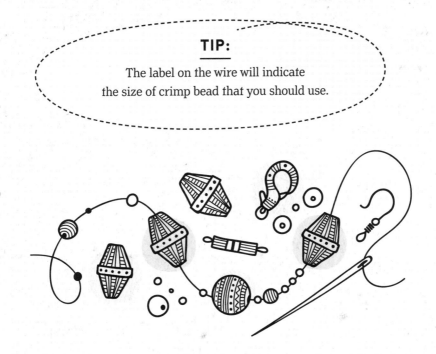

SHOES, BAGS, BELTS AND PURSES

Leather and animal-derived glues are commonly used to make many of these accessories, but nowadays it is much easier to swap them for cruelty-free alternatives. Vegan items are available to suit every budget, from high-street to high-end fashion.

Shoes

Vegan shoes are big business. Dr. Martens and Birkenstock have vegan designs; high-street brands (including ASOS and Zara) and dedicated online outlets also offer them, so whatever your budget or style, you'll be sure to find something that suits you. In high-street stores check out the labels and avoid the leather symbols (see below – suede shoes carry these symbols too). The only problem here is that it's difficult to know whether animal glue has been used, so to find a truly vegan shoe, you'll need to look for the Vegan trademark or pick a cruelty-free brand.

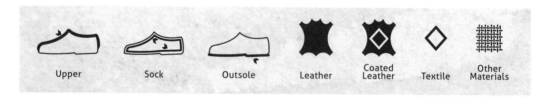

| Upper | Sock | Outsole | Leather | Coated Leather | Textile | Other Materials |

Sadly, many people believe that leather is just a by-product of the meat industry. If you would like to find out more about debunking this myth, all of the major vegan websites include links and information, but bear in mind that these can be harrowing.

Bags, Belts and Watch Straps

As with shoes, you'll want to avoid leather and animal-derived glues for a truly vegan bag, belt or watch – a quick online search for 'vegan leather bags/belts', etc. will direct you to the many options available. If you've money to spare and you want the leather look, you can treat yourself to high-end products made from cork, apple fibres, grape leather, teak leather or even recycled rubber from car manufacture.

Purses and Wallets

This category is easy: there are plenty of alternatives here, from PU (synthetic polyurethane 'leather') to fabric options, which are stocked in most high-street stores. Leather-look wallets are an alternative, too – or go for other materials, such as cork, canvas and even metal.

How to Spot Real Leather

Second-hand items may not be labelled so how can you tell if your item is leather or not? Apart from smelling it, you can check the edges – rough for real leather and smooth for imitation – and its surface for wrinkles and imperfections, which indicate it is animal-derived. Finally, dropping a little water on the item can be useful – although this may not be an option in-store! – as leather will absorb the liquid, while vegan alternatives won't.

VegaN

CHAPTER FIVE

THE VEGAN BATHROOM

There's plenty you can do to make your personal care as cruelty-free as possible – including making your own products. By veganising your bathroom one item at a time, you'll get the opportunity to make eco-friendly choices, which contain fewer unpleasant chemicals. As we come into contact with these products on a daily basis, it's good to know that vegan options are not only a compassionate alternative, but also include fewer irritants or ingredients that might be harmful to our health.

The Cruelty-free Cabinet

As with other household products, there are two things to bear in mind when you're shopping for vegan toiletries: the ingredients and the product's manufacturing history, i.e. whether it has been tested on animals. Although in the case of cosmetics and toiletries this practice has been banned in many countries, big-name companies may still have tested their products – or their individual ingredients – on animals in China (as this is a legal requirement for sales there). Vegans prefer to avoid buying these items, so looking out for a cruelty-free product pedigree is still important. Luckily, as veganism has become more mainstream, retailers are offering a wider choice of clearly labelled goods. Some of the toiletries that you're already using may well be vegan, and even some supermarket own-brand shampoos and shower gels carry the vegan label. Here's what to look for when you're stocking your bathroom cabinet.

- Cruelty-free: with toiletries and make-up labelling, this means that neither the product nor its ingredients have been tested on animals.

- Vegan: the product contains no animal-derived ingredients.

- Vegetarian: the product may include some animal by-products, such as milk, honey and beeswax.

- Organic: the product contains no harmful chemicals, and no pesticides have been used to grow the ingredients.*

- Natural: this can apply to any product that includes even a small amount of a natural ingredient. These items may well contain non-vegan elements.

*Note: This is not a legally binding term and it may be used wrongly by manufacturers.

And remember that the Vegan Society's sunflower trademark, the V-Label and the Certified Vegan Logo mean that the product is free of animal-derived ingredients AND hasn't been tested on animals either.

No-go Ingredients

Ingredient	What is it?
Beeswax	An ingredient found in sunscreen, mascara and other make-up products
Biotin	A texturiser, often derived from milk, used in hair products of all types
Carmine/cochineal/ E120/ natural red 4/C.I. 75470	This red colourant is used in lipsticks, nail polishes and blushers, and thousands of insects are crushed to produce just a few grams of it
Casein	A milk product that crops up in toiletries
Cetyl alcohol*	A wax found in hair products that may be taken from the head cavities of sea mammals
Collagen (gelatine)	Made from the tendons, ligaments and bones of various animals and fish, this is found in shampoos, face masks and beauty products
Elastin	An animal protein used in make-up and skincare products
Glycerine*	An animal fat that is found in soaps and haircare products
Guanine	Used in sparkly make-up products, this is derived from fish scales
Honey	An ingredient in shampoos, conditioners and bath products
Hyaluronic acid	Used in shampoos to add moisture to dry hair, this often comes from the umbilical cords and joints of various animals
Keratin	A common ingredient in shampoos and hair masks, this comes from the ground-up hooves, feathers and hair of various animals
Lanolin	Found in shaving creams and lotions (as well as lip products and moisturisers), it comes from sheep's wool
NAG (N-Acetyl Glucosamine)	Derived from the cells of crustaceans, this is used in skin treatments to even out skin tone
Oleic acid* (oleyl stearate; oleyl oleate; tallow)	An animal fat used in soaps
Shellac	As well as being a common ingredient in nail polish, this bug resin is used in hairspray, too
Snail gel	May be used in lotions and creams; snails are starved so that they'll produce this in greater quantities
Squalene*	Taken from sharks; this is used in deodorants (as well as moisturisers and anti-ageing products)
Stearic acid*	Derived from the stomachs of pigs and cattle, this is used in the production of soaps, deodorants and hair products

*Note: Plant-based versions of these ingredients are available, so if a product containing these is marked vegan, it will be that variety that has been used.

VEGAN-FRIENDLY PRODUCTS

Shampoos, Conditioners, Shower Gels and Bath Products

Reading the label is your first port of call, but if you're not sure about the ingredients, try a searchable online database (such as the one on the PETA website) to double-check. Go for one of the trusted brands (see opposite) or make your own natural products.

Coconut Milk Shampoo or Body Wash

Mix 60 ml full-fat coconut milk with half a cup of liquid Castile soap (such as Dr Bronner's) in a repurposed bottle. Add a few drops of your favourite essential oil for fragrance and shake well before using.

Deodorants

Some contain beeswax and glycerine, and many are tested on animals and include aluminium, too. Avoid contact with these ingredients and shop online for vegan deodorants or check out a list of safe brands before you buy. You could try a crystal deodorant stick, which just contains natural minerals, or even make your own product to avoid the chemical nasties.

DIY Deodorant

Tap into the natural antibacterial properties of tea tree oil. Dilute it in a carrier oil – such as jojoba – and do a patch test before applying under your arms. Alternatively, make it into a spray by mixing equal parts of distilled water and witch hazel in a small spray bottle, before adding in half a dozen drops of the tea tree oil. Baking powder applied with a (vegan) make-up brush is another option.

Soaps

Soaps are made from fats and oils, so it's important to check that these aren't animal-derived (opt for plant- or nut-oil-based soaps instead). The Body Shop, Dr Bronner's and Lush offer plenty of vegan-friendly options.

Toothpaste and Mouthwash

Traditional toothpaste can include glycerine (which may or may not come from animals) and propolis, among other things – and animal testing is an issue here with many of the big-brand companies – so your best option is a certified vegan choice. (The same is true for mouthwash.) Nature's Gate and Dr Bronner's are vegan-friendly options, as well as Superdrug's own-brand products. Good vegan ingredients to look out for include baking soda, stevia (in paste) and tea tree oil (in mouthwash).

Make Your Own Mouthwash

Wintergreen oil naturally neutralises odour-causing bacteria and soothes sore gums. It freshens your breath, too, so it's a perfect mouthwash ingredient. Just add a couple of drops to half a glass of water and gargle, then rinse.

Trail-blazing Brands

Some brands are synonymous with cruelty-free, ethically produced products and offer a variety of vegan-friendly choices, so keep an eye out for these, too.

+ Beauty Without Cruelty – one of the first beauty businesses to champion ethical beauty, their products are 100 per cent vegan and cruelty-free.

+ Lush – around 80 per cent of Lush products are vegan; the rest contain ingredients such as honey or beeswax, but these are clearly labelled, and the company's eco credentials are top notch too.

+ The Body Shop – around half of their products are vegan (and the website and shop staff make it easy to shop vegan) and none are tested on animals. The Body Shop blazes a trail as an eco-friendly business and is campaigning for a global ban on animal testing.

THE ECO-FRIENDLY BATHROOM

While you're streamlining your bathroom products, see if you can also make it a more eco-friendly environment. Veganising your lifestyle is all about seeing the bigger picture and these types of choices have an impact on wildlife too – whether it's a creature's environment that is affected in order to produce our raw materials or the dangers encountered by the creatures themselves, who might ingest or get tangled up in the plastics that we throw away. Here are a few areas where you might be able to lighten your ecological footprint.

Think about how items are **packaged** and reduce wrapping wherever possible.

Replace plastic items, such as toothbrushes and sponges, with **bamboo** instead.

Next time you're refitting your bathroom, go for **energy-efficient LED lights**, an extractor fan with a timer and a **low-flow showerhead**, if these are within your budget.

Install a **low-flow toilet** to save water every time you flush (or drop a plastic bottle weighed down with a few large pebbles into your tank as a speedy and cheap solution).

Turn down the temperature on your water heater.

Buy a **non-PVC shower curtain** next time you need a new one.

Use **recycled loo paper**.

Give up disposable razors and opt instead for a **metal safety razor** with blades. (Collect used blades in a safe place and take to your nearest metal recycling point.)

Don't use expensive, chemical-laden **bathroom cleaning products** – sprinkle baking soda on the area you need to clean, pour on a little white vinegar and leave for 10 minutes, before cleaning off with an eco-friendly cloth. (You can always add essential oil to give your bathroom a less vinegary scent!)

Keep **the water that you run off** while waiting to get your shower to the right temperature and use it for cleaning, watering the plants or flushing the loo.

Swap **shaving foam** or liquid soap for a rich bar of plant-oil-based soap.

Reuse or **recycle** the empty **containers** of your bath products.

PERSONAL CARE

Animal-derived products can make their way into the most intimate areas of our lives, but a little research can help you to find the most ethical option that works for you.

Menstrual Products

This is an area where single-use plastics are a big issue. With the average woman using anything from 11,000 to 16,000 menstrual products in their lifetime – and these items taking around 500 years to break down – this is an area where ethical shopping makes an enormous difference. Big-brand companies have a bad history in terms of animal testing here, too, and the dioxins in most mainstream products are potentially harmful to humans as well as the environment. Here are some ethical options, and the good news is that many are the same price, if not cheaper, than traditional brands.

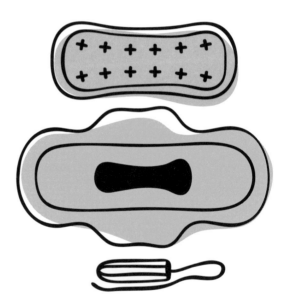

- 100 per cent cotton sanitary products – check out Time of the Month and Natracare, but you'll find more options online.

- Washable, reusable sanitary towels – there are lots of these on Etsy, but make sure you opt for cotton rather than wool or silk.

- A menstrual cup – these last for up to ten years. Mooncup and Lena are tried-and-trusted brands (look online for plenty of reviews and links for these).

Birth Control

This is something that many people don't even contemplate when they first become vegan, but there are a few things you can take into consideration.

- Most condoms, which are made from latex, contain casein and are not vegan. However, vegan brands do exist, such as Glyde or Sir Richard's (whose products are donated to developing countries in return for sales) – and even Durex sell vegan options. (Note: In the UK all Boots own-brand condoms are vegan.)

- For diaphragms, you'll need to avoid latex and go for silicone, but lubricants and spermicides will need to be sourced from a certified vegan brand.

- Birth control pills don't have great vegan credentials, as all have been tested on animals and many contain milk derivatives, but they may be the best option for you.

- IUDs do not have a cruelty-free history, but a non-hormonal device – which is simply a copper filament around a polyethylene implant – doesn't include any non-vegan elements.

Remember that it is virtually impossible to live a 100 per cent vegan lifestyle and there are some areas where you may need to make a few compromises. Many people need to use hormone-based products, so if this applies to you, bear in mind that you are still living your life in the most ethical way possible – don't beat yourself up if this is an area in which you can't be 'perfect'!

Medicines and Supplements

Your medicine cabinet is probably the trickiest area of your life to veganise, as all medicines must be tested before they can be licensed, but there is still a lot you can do to make ethical choices. If you're treating minor ailments, natural remedies from plants and herbs could help (see pp.138–139 for some ideas). Alternatively, the Vegan Society offers a list of commonly used meds that don't contain any animal derivatives, so check these before your next trip to the pharmacy.

If you are prescribed a medicine, have a chat with your healthcare professional to see what's available. You can check out their ingredients on www.medicines.org.uk or via the FDA search engine in the US, but you may need to do some further research and contact the manufacturer, as it might not be clear whether certain components are plant- or animal-derived.

Tips When Checking Medication

✦ Non-vegan components include: gelatine, lactose, shellac, glycocholic acid and magnesium stearate (the latter can come from plants, too).

✦ Capsules are likely to contain gelatine, so often aren't the best vegan option.

✦ Tablets that contain sucrose could be vegan, as this is often used in place of lactose.

✦ You may find that consulting a specially trained plant-based practitioner will help. Try www.plantbaseddoctors.org to find someone local to you.

- You may find that there are no alternatives to taking medicines that contain animal derivatives – in these cases remember that veganism is a commitment to pursuing a vegan lifestyle as far as is practical for you. Medication is a notoriously tricky area – but by making vegan choices in other spheres of your life, the positive impact you are having will far outweigh any compromises that you may need to make here. Always talk to your doctor if you have any concerns about your medication – and never stop or change prescriptions without taking their advice first.

Supplements

Taking supplements is less of a minefield, as many are produced with vegans in mind and there are numerous plant-based brands out there. It's safest to stick to these, as other types can include animal-derived components. As well as the ingredients listed on pp.44–45, others to avoid or investigate include:

- Carotene
- Chondroitin
- Fatty acids
- Fish oil
- Glucosamine
- Glutamic acid
- Hyaluronic acid
- Lecithin
- Linoleic acid
- Lipase
- Oestrogen
- Propolis
- Progesterone
- Steroids
- Tyrosine
- Vitamins A, D3 and B12*

*These can come from plant or animal sources, so you may need to double-check if you're unsure.

NATURAL HEALTH-CARE

Plants are nature's medicine cabinet – a wonderful, pure and powerful source of natural compounds that can heal and soothe. Herbal remedies have been around for centuries and are the ultimate vegan medicine, so it's well worth giving them a try if you're suffering from minor aches and gripes.

Painkillers

Foodstuffs that have natural analgesic qualities include: berries and cherries, ginger, apple cider vinegar (raw and unprocessed – mix 2 tsp in a cup of water and drink), olives, beetroot, papaya and cayenne. All of these contain substances that have been shown to reduce pain and often inflammation too. Experiment and see which are most effective for you.

Period Pain and Menstrual Issues

Turmeric is a powerful antioxidant that helps to regulate periods and combat period pain. Make your own turmeric tea and drink a cup every day of the month: add 1 tsp turmeric to a saucepan of boiling water and simmer for 10 minutes. Pour into a cup, leaving behind the dregs, and top with a little cold water to cool. Serve with a dash of agave syrup, 1 tsp coconut oil or a sprinkle of black pepper for a spicy tea.

Cold and Flu Remedy

Drink hot water with lemon and ginger or boil some broccoli and drink the cooking water, which will be full of vitamins. Sage tea is also great for a sore throat; echinacea works well too, while boosting the immune system at the same time.

Acne Treatment

Add a dash of apple cider vinegar or a few drops of tea tree oil to 60 ml of water and apply to your face with a cotton wool ball. Rinse off with cold water.

Indigestion Remedy

When it comes to soothing digestive troubles, peppermint and liquorice root are both good – you can buy the latter at most health food stores and simply chew it, or chop it into pieces and use as an alternative to chewing gum after meals. You could also buy (or grow) peppermint and make your own tea by adding boiling water to the leaves.

Muscle Rub

Massage a few drops of wintergreen oil into the area for speedy pain relief. Wintergreen is another natural anti-inflammatory, which can also be used for cold and flu relief – just mix a few drops with coconut oil, and rub on your chest and neck to combat congestion.

Sleep Tonic

If you're struggling to sleep, try chamomile or valerian tea. You could also have a glass of warm cherry juice (cherries are a natural source of melatonin, which regulates your sleep cycle) or eat a handful of almonds (for magnesium) and a couple of Brazil nuts (for selenium), which will help you to sleep better.

Herbal Helpers

Soothe sunburn, insect bites and minor skin ailments with aloe vera gel. The best source is a plant on your windowsill: just break open a leaf when you need some first aid. Melted coconut oil has antibacterial qualities, so use to treat cuts and blisters (or mouth ulcers, by swilling – and spitting out – a tablespoon of oil). Ginger and activated charcoal (in the form of tablets) are great for easing nausea and digestive complaints.

NOT
TESTED ON
ANIMALS

CHAPTER SIX

VEGAN BEAUTY

Cruelty-free beauty is big news, and today's vegan products are mainstream and easy to track down. From skincare and make-up to perfumes and body art there's a compassionate option out there to suit your budget – and if you want to be 100 per cent plant-based when it comes to the products you use on your skin, you can always try your hand at making your own.

CRUELTY-FREE MAKE-UP AND BEAUTY

Beauty products are another area where there are two issues to consider: animal testing and ingredients. Big-name companies may have tested make-up or skincare products on animals overseas, so look for 'cruelty-free' or vegan labelling – or the Leaping Bunny or Vegan Society logos – to guide you.

When it comes to ingredients, fewer additives are better for your skin – and your brain, if you find yourself working your way through ingredients lists and checking each item out! (The table on pp.43–44 lists the most regular offenders to avoid.) **Collagen** and **elastin** are an obvious no-no in face creams, and **carmine (cochineal)** is a common red colourant used

in make-up products. Look out for **guanine** in anything sparkly or shiny (such as eye shadows and bronzers) and, of course, **shellac** in nail polishes.

The good news is that vegan make-up and skincare products tend to be very gentle and much kinder to the skin, using far fewer additives, and – thanks to the huge market trend towards ethical beauty products – there are plenty of options available to suit all budgets. The own-brand range at your local chemist could well be a vegan option. Check out vegan beauty blogs online, too, for reviews of products that appeal to you.

Product Detective

It's not always easy to work out what's in your beauty products. Even if all the ingredients are listed, the details are often tricky to read. The searchable cosmetics database at www.ewg.org is a useful resource that details the components of most popular cosmetics and skincare products. Clicking on individual ingredients will give you more information about them – it often lists animal-derived items with cross-references to the PETA website, but you may still need to do a little detective work to discover if your product is truly vegan.

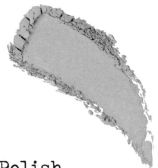

Nail Polish

Most 'standard' nail polish is not vegan, but this has led to cruelty-free companies developing their own, beautiful, vegan ranges. Beauty Without Cruelty, Manic Panic and Urban Decay are just a few examples, but there are dozens more to discover via beauty blogs or good old Google.

Vegan-friendly Make-up and Beauty Brands

When you're replacing items in your make-up bag, these vegan-friendly brands are a good place to start. (Remember that your local pharmacy may well have vegan products to offer too.)

B.

Barry M.*

Beauty Without Cruelty

The Body Shop

Kat Von D*

Lush*

Pacifica

skyn ICELAND

Urban Decay*

wet n wild*

*Not all of these brands' products are 100 per cent vegan, but they are at least vegetarian and cruelty-free.

MAKE-UP TOOLS AND EXTRAS

Make-up Brushes

Brushes were traditionally made from animal hair and many still are, but luckily the easily findable vegan alternatives are not only cruelty-free, but more hygienic too. The Body Shop, EcoTools and Urban Decay are just a few of the brands to look for, which also produce their ranges in an eco-friendly way. (The Urban Decay brushes are made in part from recycled bottles.)

Sponges

For make-up sponges and blenders, most of the vegan-friendly companies offer ethical options (Beautyblender items are a good choice too).

Eyelashes

False eyelashes can be made from mink, but synthetic sets are produced by most vegan-friendly make-up brands. Ardell, e.l.f. and Unicorn Cosmetics offer good, affordable options.

Wipes, Cotton Wool and Cotton Buds (Q-tips)

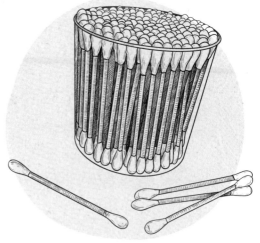

Cotton wool balls and pads are made from cotton or synthetic fibres, but the production of non-organic cotton is detrimental to the environment and the fact that all of these items are single-use means that they don't have a great eco-profile. Buying organic cotton pads – or alternatives made from soft bamboo and hemp – is one option. Even better, you could use a muslin cloth, washable cleansing pad or a konjac sponge – or make your own washable pads from circles of old towels or fleece fabric.

Swap plastic cotton buds (Q-tips) for bamboo or paper-based ones (available in most high-street stores) and compost these or put them with your other organic waste. (Do not flush them down the toilet.)

NATURAL SKINCARE

One way of guaranteeing that you're using truly natural, 100 per cent vegan skincare products on your body is to make your own. Your home-made goodies will be more eco-friendly and much kinder to your skin, so get your repurposed bottles ready and mix up your own vegan skincare range.

Make-up Remover

Mix one part olive oil or jojoba oil with one part witch hazel (a vegan-friendly version of the latter is easy to source online) for a make-up remover that will gently lift products off your skin. Witch hazel is good for treating irritated skin and managing breakouts, too.

Cleanse

Oil-cleansing is a simple and very popular method. Just massage castor oil (or coconut oil) into your skin, leave for 30 seconds and then wash off with a warm cloth. It may take a few days for your skin to adjust to your new regime, so give this method a try for a couple of weeks or so to see if it suits you.

Exfoliate

For a gentle exfoliating cleanser, add 3 tbsp rice milk to 60 g rice flour and mix into a paste. Massage into your face and then rinse off with warm water. For something with a little more exfoliating power, mix 120 ml olive oil into 200 g brown sugar and add in a few drops of your favourite essential oil for fragrance.

Tone

Mix one part apple cider vinegar with two parts water, and shake. Apply to your face and leave to dry before moisturising.

Hair Mask

Blend one mashed banana with half an avocado and squeeze in the juice of half a lemon. Mix thoroughly and apply to your hair, leaving for half an hour before rinsing off with cool water.

Lip Scrub

For a super-easy lip scrub simply stir 1 tsp olive oil into 1 tbsp brown sugar. Or how about taking a couple of tablespoons of used coffee grounds and mixing in 2 tsp of coconut oil? Add a few drops of peppermint or vanilla essential oil and store your lip scrub in the fridge.

LUXURIOUS AVOCADO FACE MASK

Avocados are packed with goodness, and they're great for your skin too. For a super-easy moisturiser, eat an avocado and then apply the residue from the inside of the skin to your face. Leave for 10 minutes and rinse off with warm water. For a more sophisticated, luxurious treatment, try mixing up this mask.

You will need:
1 avocado

1 tsp olive oil

1 tsp lemon juice

juice of half an orange

1. Mash the avocado in a bowl and add the olive oil, lemon juice and orange juice.

2. Mix and apply the mask to your face after cleansing (avoiding your eye area).

3. Relax for 20–30 minutes while the mask works its magic.

4. Rinse off thoroughly using warm water and then close your pores by splashing with cold water.

PERFUMES, DYES AND BODY DÉCOR

Perfumes and Aftershaves

The only sure-fire way to find vegan scents is to purchase certified brands, as manufacturers aren't obliged to list their ingredients on the packaging. Many well-known labels use animal-derived musks to make perfumes last and – of course – animal testing is sadly an issue. There are a multitude of vegan perfume companies out there, though, and high-street shops such as The Body Shop, H&M and Lush also carry vegan-friendly alternatives. There are dozens of online reviews and handy lists of options to suit every budget. (In the UK, check out the M&S website for their 'suitable for vegans' range of scents.)

Ingredients to Avoid in Scents

- ◆ Ambergris (which is derived from the intestine of sperm whales)
- ◆ Castoreum (a scent-marking substance secreted by beavers)
- ◆ Civet (a scent-marker produced by civet wildcats)
- ◆ Honey
- ◆ Leather
- ◆ Milk
- ◆ Musk (originally taken from musk deer, nowadays this can be synthetically sourced, but check specific brands online)

Hair

A trip to the hairdresser, barber or beauty salon can be a challenge when it comes to pursuing your veganised lifestyle. The products they use may not come from a cruelty-free company and it's almost impossible to check out the ingredients for everything that your stylist uses. Calling ahead first to get the low-down on the brands that they use is a good start – or if you find a local vegan-friendly establishment, that's even better. Most hair dyes contain animal derivatives, but some salons – such as Paul Mitchell – offer vegan alternatives. This is a case for some tough detective work!

Tattoos

When it comes to vegan-friendly body art, the inks are your first consideration – some may contain glycerine, gelatine or shellac – but finding an artist who uses vegan-friendly ones is not too tricky. A more complicated area can be the other materials and aftercare products that the studio uses – from stencils (containing lanolin) and razors (with glycerine strips) to soaps and balms. The website vegantattoostudios.com can help, or you could give your local establishment a call to discuss your requirements. If the inks are vegan friendly, you may be able to find a good compromise by bringing along some of your own products.

TAKING IT FURTHER

If you've veganised your lifestyle and want to go one step further, there are always opportunities to promote vegan causes and to inspire or educate others to make compassionate choices, too.

Give a talk at a local club.

Start a blog about your choices and share your new knowledge.

Set up a vegan Meetup group or coffee meet.

Attend a march or protest.

Support an animal rights charity.

Take vegan bakes to every social event you attend!

Take part in a vigil.

Campaign to veganise the menu in your work (or school) canteen.

Get a vegan job (check out veganjobs.com)!

Organise a World Vegan Day celebration.

GLOSSARY

Accidentally vegan – a term for everyday food items that happen to be vegan.

Animal derivatives – ingredients or substances that come from animals.

Certified organic – an organic product that has been accredited.

Cruelty-free – in labelling, this means that a product hasn't been tested on animals (but it may still contain animal derivatives).

Ethical – used to describe products that have been produced without the exploitation of animals, humans or the environment.

Flexitarian – someone who eats a largely vegan or vegetarian diet, but occasionally eats fish or meat.

Fragrance-free – a product that has not had an artificial scent added to it, although it may carry the natural scent of its ingredients.

Free-range – animals living in free-range conditions should have access to the outdoors, but this is seldom the case in practice.

Freegan – a person (often vegan) who only eats food that they've grown or found, usually in protest against capitalism.

Natural – often used to describe the ingredients in beauty products, this term may not apply to all the ingredients and doesn't mean that the product is vegan.

Nooch – vegan slang for nutritional yeast.

Nutritional yeast – a much-loved vegan ingredient that brings cheesy-flavoured goodness (and vitamin B12) to vegan cooking.

Omnivore – someone who eats all types of foods, including meat and dairy.

Organic – a product that has been grown without the use of synthetic fertilisers, pesticides or hormones.

Ovo-lacto vegetarian – someone who doesn't eat meat or fish, but does eat eggs and dairy products.

Pescatarian – someone who doesn't eat meat but does eat fish.

Raw vegan – vegans who only consume raw foods.

Seitan – a high-protein alternative to meat, made from cooked wheat gluten.

Sustainable – a term used to describe materials that are taken from a source that is responsibly managed and replenished, so that levels won't go down over time.

Tempeh – fermented soya beans that can be used in place of meat.

Tofu – a curd made from mashed soya beans; a staple in the vegan kitchen.

Vegan (adjective) – a foodstuff or item that doesn't include any animal-derived components and hasn't been tested on animals.

Vegan (noun) – a person who chooses not to use or consume anything that comes from animals (or has been tested on them), and an all-round compassionate human being .

Veganic gardening – gardening without using any chemicals or animal-derived products.

Vegetarian – someone who doesn't eat meat or fish, but usually eats eggs and dairy products.

RESOURCES

Organisations

The Vegan Awareness Foundation (Vegan Action) – an organisation that works hard to raise awareness of animal rights issues by organising events, and running campaigns and outreach programmes.

The Vegan Society – a registered charity that has been educating the world about veganism since 1944. Their website is a wealth of information on everything from how to go vegan to campaign news and recipes.

Veganuary – a charity that inspires people to give veganism a try in January and aims to support them to transition to a vegan lifestyle in the long term. They are a wonderful resource for information, advice and encouragement.

The Vegetarian Resource Group – an organisation that educates people about vegetarianism, with a useful website full of recipes and other information.

PETA – this animal rights organisation is dedicated to campaigning for the protection of animals worldwide. Their website includes plenty of information on veganism and the difference that being vegan makes.

10 Brilliant Vegan Blogs

There are so many inspirational vegan and vegetarian blogs out there. Here are just a few to get you started.

Brownble – educational and aspirational, this blog contains lots of info on cooking vegan.

Eco-Vegan Gal – practical tips on living a cruelty-free, eco-friendly lifestyle.

Ethical Elephant – a super-informative vegan lifestyle blog.

The Flaming Vegan – a community blog covering everything from gardening to nutrition.

Naturally Ella – a blog packed with seasonal vegetarian recipes.

Oh She Glows – lovely vegan recipes with inspirational pictures.

Plant Positive Running – a blog that combines tips on plant-based eating and running.

Urban Vegan – reviews and recommendations for every type of vegan product.

Vegan Beauty Review – brilliant blog with lots of advice on cruelty-free beauty.

Vegan Womble – a vegan community blog packed with info on every aspect of veganism.

Websites

The internet is an absolutely brilliant resource with a plethora of useful websites and material to guide you on every aspect of plant-based living. Apart from the websites for the organisations listed on the previous page, take a look at the following.

www.plantbasednews.org – up-to-date news on vegan issues, with reviews and interviews too.

www.vivahealth.org.uk – a great resource of vegan health and nutritional information.

www.meetup.com – search your local area for vegan groups and events.

www.barnivore.com – an online directory of vegan wine, beer and spirits.

thegoodshoppingguide.com – for checking out ethically sourced furniture. It compares furniture outlets and rates them, with a traffic-light system, for timber sourcing, animal welfare, human rights, etc.

www.greenchoices.org – advice on how to make ethical choices in every area of your life.

www.treehugger.com – full of practical advice on eco-friendly living.

vegandesign.org – a wealth of information about vegan and ethical interior design.

veganjobs.com – a global database of vegan-friendly jobs.

www.compassionatecloset.com/blogs/wearnoharm/63049091-cruelty-free-fabric-guide – a handy database of vegan fabrics.

www.plantbaseddoctors.org – a great global tool for finding vegan-friendly practitioners.

vegandoctors.co.uk – a website that aims to improve education around plant-based health.

www.medicines.org.uk – an up-to-date database of medicines used in the UK.

www.ewg.org – a group that works to research and inform consumers about environmental issues and what is in the products we use.

vegantattoostudios.com – a database to help you find a vegan tattoo studio near you.

Inspirational Documentaries

These documentaries are hard-hitting but super-informative.

Earthlings – exposes the reality of animal agriculture using undercover footage.
Forks Over Knives – explores the health benefits of plant-based eating.
Vegucated – three NY omnivores go vegan and discover the truth about the meat industry.
Live and Let Live – a documentary that explores the reasons for going vegan.
Cowspiracy – reveals the negative link between animal agriculture and the environment.

Top Vegan Apps and Web Tools

With these handy apps and tools just a click away, you'll have every aspect of vegan living sorted.

21-Day Vegan Kickstart – a recipe-planning app to ease you into plant-based eating.
Bunny Free – app offered by PETA to check if products are cruelty-free.
Forks Over Knives – a recipe and nutrition app to guide you into veganism.
HappyCow – find vegan food in your area.
Is It Vegan? – handy product scanner to find out if items are vegan.
The Vegan Calculator – an app that shows how your new vegan lifestyle could benefit the environment.
The Vegan Passport – useful app for helping you communicate your vegan needs when eating abroad.
Vegaholic – a useful app for when you're out on the town. It uses a traffic-light system to classify whether or not a drink is vegan friendly.
Veganalyser – an app that works out how many animals you could save by going vegan.
vegEMOJI – don't just fill your store cupboard with veggies – fill your phone with them too!
VNutrition – keep track of your daily nutrients and make sure you're not missing out.

CONCLUSION

These are just a few of the resources that you can tap into to help you explore a vegan lifestyle – and I hope that you enjoy your journey. I'm sure you'll encounter many exciting recipes and products... and perhaps find some previously hidden cooking or crafting skills, too. Above all, enjoy being part of a friendly and supportive global community, and remember that every compassionate choice you're able to make has a positive impact on wildlife and the environment. You're doing a wonderful thing by exploring vegan living!

Image Credits

Cover images – front panel © lena_nikolaeva/
Shutterstock.com; back panel: shoes © Kostiantyn
Ablazov; soap © Syda Productions/Shutterstock.com;
lounge © Photographee.eu/Shutterstock.com; shopper
© DavideAngelini/Shutterstock.com

pp.4/5 – trainers © bracelet © Yuliia Bahniuk/
Shutterstock.com; chair © Iliveinoctober/Shutterstock.
com; shirt, salad and lettuce © Rin Ohara/
Shutterstock.com

p.7 © Libellule/Shutterstock.com

p.8 © SehrguteFotos/Shutterstock.com

p.9 © Foxys Forest Manufacture/Shutterstock.com

p.10 – globe © Sloth Astronaut/Shutterstock.com; car ©
Laura Reyero/Shutterstock.com

p.11 – leaves © Maksym Godlevskyi/Shutterstock.com;
whale © By Aliona LUK/Shutterstock.com

p.13 © one line man/Shutterstock.com

pp.14/15 © By lena_nikolaeva/Shutterstock.com

p.16 – avocado © SEE D JAN/Shutterstock.com;
blueberries © Evdokimov Maxim/Shutterstock.com;
kale © Elena Elisseeva/Shutterstock.com; mushrooms
© AleksandarMilutinovic/Shutterstock.com

p.17 – nuts © yesyesterday/Shutterstock.com; pulses
© Alina Yudina/Shutterstock.com; seaweed ©
Valentina_G/Shutterstock.com; sweet potatoes ©
AnjelikaGr/Shutterstock.com; turmeric © tarapong
srichaiyos/Shutterstock.com

p.19 © Litvinova Elena Sergeevna/Shutterstock.com

p.20 ©Photographee.eu/Shutterstock.com

p.21 © lena_nikolaeva/Shutterstock.com

p.22 © kondratya/Shutterstock.com

p.23 © Ilya Bolotov/Shutterstock.com

p.25 burger © Chris Allan/Shutterstock.com; falafel ©
Alphonsine Sabine/Shutterstock.com

pp.26/27 © Feliche Vero/Shutterstock.com

p.28 – table © fire_fly/Shutterstock.com; bus © Dmitry
Shanchuk/Shutterstock.com; thermostat © Dzm1try/

Shutterstock.com; windfarm © yuRomanovich/
Shutterstock.com

p.29 – teapot © MarCh13/Shutterstock.com;
bottles © shopplaywood/Shutterstock.com;
apple © Barry Barnes/Shutterstock.com; wipes ©
TopVectorElements/Shutterstock.com; jar © Nikitina
Karina/Shutterstock.com

p.32 © melazerg/Shutterstock.com

p.34 © Foxys Forest Manufacture/Shutterstock.com

pp.36/37 – nuts and seeds © Po-melkomy/Shutterstock.
com; fruit © Angelina De Sol/Shutterstock.com;
legumes © uladzimir zgurski/Shutterstock.com;
vegetables © primiaou/Shutterstock.com; grains and
starchy veggies © mahmuttibet/Shutterstock.com;
triangle © Tomas Florian/Shutterstock.com

pp.38/39 © rzarek/Shutterstock.com

p.40 © arirukuchika/Shutterstock.com

p.42 © LanaN/Shutterstock.com

p.43 © DavideAngelini/Shutterstock.com

p.44 © Lemonade Serenade/Shutterstock.com

p.46 © Lia Li/Shutterstock.com

pp.48/49 – pancakes © Ester Sall/Shutterstock.com;
Chia pot © Lara Uster/Shutterstock.com; oats ©
Fascinadora/Shutterstock.com; avocado © Africa
Studio/Shutterstock.com

p.50 © muh23/Shutterstock.com

pp.52/53 © Maryna_R/Shutterstock.com

p.55 © By Anna_Pustynnikova/Shutterstock.com

p.56 © Natalya Levish/Shutterstock.com

p.59 © rzarek/Shutterstock.com

p.60 © Visual Generation/Shutterstock.com

p.61 © conssuella/Shutterstock.com

pp.62/63 © Rin Ohara/Shutterstock.com

p.64 © Galiyah Assan/Shutterstock.com

p.66 © Swedish Marble/Shutterstock.com

p.69 © Elena Veselova/Shutterstock.com

p.70 © Fribus Mara/Shutterstock.com

p.71 © Meow Wanvilai/Shutterstock.com

p.72 © hayashi_chan/Shutterstock.com

p.73 © Irina Vaneeva/Shutterstock.com

p.77 © MaraZe/Shutterstock.com

p.78 © Rin Ohara/Shutterstock.com

p.80 © Moloko88/Shutterstock.com

p.81 © one line man/Shutterstock.com

p.82 © Askhat Gilyakhov/Shutterstock.com

p.83 © kondratya/Shutterstock.com

pp.84/85 © HAKINMHAN/Shutterstock.com

pp.86/87 © Nikitina Karina/Shutterstock.com

p.88 © UfaBizPhoto/Shutterstock.com

p.89 – ironing board © y Kitch Bain/Shutterstock.com

p.90 © Maryna_R/Shutterstock.com

pp.92/93 – throw © Photographee.eu/Shutterstock.com; rug © Jodie Johnson/Shutterstock.com; cushion © VDB Photos/Shutterstock.com; sofa © WorldWide/Shutterstock.com

p.94 – chair © Iliveinoctober/Shutterstock.com; leaf and recycle icon © pashabo/Shutterstock.com

pp.96/97 © Nikitina Karina/Shutterstock.com

pp.98/99 © Photographee.eu/Shutterstock.com

pp.100/101 © antpkr/Shutterstock.com

p.103 © Liga Cerina/Shutterstock.com

p.104 © Julia August/Shutterstock.com

p.105 © Drawlab19/Shutterstock.com

p.106 © Anna Elesina/Shutterstock.com

p.107 – pad © kak2s/Shutterstock.com; paw © Julia August/Shutterstock.com

p.108 © mubus7/Shutterstock.com

p.109 © nada54/Shutterstock.com

p.110 © Morinka/Shutterstock.com

p.111 © By FernPat/Shutterstock.com

p.113 © By Peter Turner Photography/Shutterstock.com

p.114 © By kateka/Shutterstock.com

p.115 © rzarek/Shutterstock.com

p.117 © Rin Ohara/Shutterstock.com

p.119 – coat © Baleika Tamara/Shutterstock.com; tag © Hayati Kayhan/Shutterstock.com

pp.120/121 © gator TheArtisticLens/Shutterstock.com; glasses © Garrett Aitken/Shutterstock.com; pearls © By Kristijan Dimoski/Shutterstock.com; puffa © y aimy27feb/Shutterstock.com; buttons © MikeBraune/Shutterstock.com; hat © Protsenko_Photo/Shutterstock.com; jeans © korkeng/Shutterstock.com; broach © Victor Moussa/Shutterstock.com

p.123 © Yuliia Bahniuk/Shutterstock.com

p.124 – boots © Soloviova Liudmyla/Shutterstock.com; symbols © Cath Vectorielle/Shutterstock.com

p.125 © Still AB/Shutterstock.com

p.126 © Trish Volt/Shutterstock.com

p.128 © Elena Kazanskaya/Shutterstock.com

pp.132/133 © rzarek/Shutterstock.com

p.134 © Vera Serg/Shutterstock.com

pp.136/137 © Polar_lights/Shutterstock.com

pp.138/139 – ginger © Tina Bits/Shutterstock.com; lemon © By Plateresca/Shutterstock.com; aloe © everigenia/Shutterstock.com; nuts © koffiekup/Shutterstock.com

p.140 © john dory/Shutterstock.com

p.142 © Olga Sabarova/Shutterstock.com

p.143 © Pro3DArtt/Shutterstock.com

pp.144/145 – brushes © Sonya illustration/Shutterstock.com; sponges © Bodor Tivadar/Shutterstock.com; lashes © Vracovska/Shutterstock.com; cotton buds © chempina/Shutterstock.com

pp.146/147 © anon_tae/Shutterstock.com

p.149 © kitzzeh/Shutterstock.com

p.150 © Africa Studio/Shutterstock.com

p.151 © Mikhail_Kayl/Shutterstock.com

p.152 © Irina Vaneeva/Shutterstock.com

p.160 © Julia August/Shutterstock.com

If you're interested in finding out more about our books, find us on Facebook at **Summersdale Publishers** and follow us on Twitter at **@Summersdale**.

www.summersdale.com